SOUTHERN ROUTES

SOUTHERN ROUTES

Secret Recipes from the Best Down-Home Joints in the South

BEN VAUGHN

NELSON
BOOKS

An Imprint of Thomas Nelson

Published in Nashville, Tennessee, by Nelson Books, an imprint of Thomas Nelson. Nelson Books and Thomas Nelson are registered trademarks of HarperCollins Christian Publishing, Inc.

Photography by Sean O'Halloran

Thomas Nelson, Inc., titles may be purchased in bulk for educational, business, fund-raising, or sales promotional use. For information, please e-mail SpecialMarkets@ThomasNelson.com.

Library of Congress Control Number: 2015938278

ISBN 13: 978-0-7180-1162-8

Printed in the United States of America

15 16 17 18 19 QG 6 5 4 3 2 1

CONTENTS

Foreword

There Is Something About the South

I was raised in a small town in the industrial heartland that was the north of England. That may not seem particularly relevant to this book until I explain that it wasn't until I was in my early twenties, after I had been bitten hard by the travel bug, that the term "the South" came to mean anything to me other than a reference to Blighty's capital city, London.

Once I started journeying regularly throughout the United States, however, this all changed, and like so many other travelers before me, I soon fell in love with that beguiling land lying below the Mason-Dixon Line.

Over many vacations spent crisscrossing America, it was to the south of the country that I was (and still am) drawn. I found that states such as Georgia, Tennessee, Alabama, Louisiana, and Mississippi have so much to offer visitors, and yet they seem to receive so little love from their fellow states to the north and west.

At first it was the beauty of the rural South that drew me in. Some of my all-time happiest holiday memories include dipping my toes in the waters of the Gulf of Mexico while sipping a Shiner Bock beer in Galveston, Texas, gawping at the majestic beauty of the Smoky Mountains as I drove through East Tennessee, and catching my breath as I whizzed through the Florida Everglades on an airboat in search of a gator.

The friendliness of the people caught me by surprise, as I met folks who were as far removed from me politically, religiously, and culturally as it was possible to get, and yet who showed me a soul-nourishing hospitality that surpassed any I have encountered elsewhere in the United States, and indeed, matched any I have found in any country on the planet. I have been the recipient of countless beers as people instructed me to "sit a spell" and chat with them. I have been offered beds in places I had never heard of by people I barely knew, and I am fairly sure that I have gained twenty pounds in weight thanks to the bread I have broken at the tables of the families who insisted on sharing their meals with me.

Ah, that Southern food.

Whatever first attracts me to a region or a country, it is the quality of what I eat there that makes me decide if I am ever going to revisit. Once I began to realize just how bloody delicious the food was in the Southern states, my return to the region many, many times was never in doubt.

Over the last twenty years the South has rarely let me down when I have been in search of genuine deliciousness, and I have had to poke a couple of extra holes in my hard-working belt to testify to the po' boys I've scarfed down in New Orleans, the cracklings I have purchased along with my gas at truck stops in Texas, the fried chicken legs I have gnawed down to sawdust at Gus's in Tennessee, and the countless barbecue shops I have been lured to by the signs that draw you, like sirens, from the freeway in search of smoked meat.

Most of all, thanks to numerous visits primarily to Nashville, Tennessee, I have fallen under the spell of the "meat and three," diners that serve up slices of juicy ham, thick pork chops, or meatloaf alongside unnaturally large piles of mac 'n' cheese, corn, and green beans. Fine dining it most definitely isn't, but my first experience of this uniquely Southern meal, at Rotiers in Nashville, still remains one of my favorite dining memories, even if (whispers) I would rank sweetened ice tea up there with the rotten shark meat I ate in Iceland on the food nastiness scale.

The food of the South is experiencing a well-deserved and long overdue spell in the culinary spotlight. Chefs such as Sean Brock in Charleston, South Carolina, and Chris Hastings in Birmingham, Alabama, have shown that not only does the South have access to some of the finest ingredients, but it also has chefs who know how to use them to spectacular effect. Despite heartily applauding this recognition of talented chefs, when I think of what first attracted me to the food of the South, it is the memories of the down-home places that bring a smile to my face and make my stomach create noises that scare the neighbor's children.

That's why I was delighted when my good chum Ben Vaughn told me that his newest project would be *Southern Routes*, a book that would not only catalog the best of the best of family restaurants in the South but would also give the reader access to recipes that have kept generation after generation filled to the brim. *Southern Routes* is a book that has been crying out to be written, and I can think of no better person to write it than Ben, who may not be a natural-born native of the South, but who has taken to its culture with such passion that he almost cries sausage gravy when he talks about the South and its food.

So, as I have been asked to do on so many occasions, I urge you to sit a spell with Ben and enjoy his journey through the best joints in ten states. I guarantee it will make you crave a meat and three, and when it does, I'll see you at Rotiers.

SIMON MAJUMDAR
FOOD NETWORK ON-AIR CRITIC
LOS ANGELES, 2015

Introduction

There is something original about the concept of allowing patrons to select a single meat from a menu and then choose three vegetables. Something about this thing called a meat and three restaurant in the South feels unique when nothing else does. These restaurants have been verified by time and are genuine. The history behind Southern food is notable, romantic, and filled with love. These restaurants speak of familiarity, consistency, and personal ownership. Each one of the chairs in the dining room has a story to tell because the owners and staff have been a part of raising their communities for generations.

In *Southern Routes*, I explored my transplanted Southern roots with an edible journey that highlights some of the best-kept food secrets in the South. This journey was an adventure that I knew was for me the second I discovered that mac 'n' cheese is considered a vegetable on most Southern tables. That fact alone was enough evidence for me that I have a Southern soul.

I often say if you want your pennyworth of authentic Southern food, visit a meat and three restaurant because that is where you can find some of the most authentic food in the South.

An edible adventure through the South sounds tasty, but what was the purpose? My objective was to visit ten states, finding ten locations per state serving the best Southern foods, from peach cobbler, barbecue, chicken, pork, and fish to cornbread, peas, lima beans, greens, and hushpuppies. You think you know what Southern food is? I bet it has been set in your mind that it's only fried chicken and greens. Well, you are missing the goodies in-between. In this book I'll take you on a trip to 100 restaurants highlighting 100 of the best items, and bestow upon you one hundred recipes straight from the source. And these recipes wouldn't be complete without the family stories I discovered along the way. Getting to know the thankless cooks, chefs, owners, and managers from these iconic meat and three restaurants showed me that the memories and stories are as savory as the food.

In the South, it all begins at the supper table. For Southerners, food is comfort. Mom's black-eyed peas and buttermilk fried chicken might not change your life, but they sure are a start and certainly memorable. It's the love and attention that each simple ingredient receives that makes Southern food so remarkable. There are no impostors in a Southern kitchen; it's just the way "we" do it. It's not right or wrong; it just works. Some of my favorite examples of true Southern food break every culinary rule I've learned. But who am I to change tradition? And why would I want to when it tastes so good?

In most of my experiences during my travels for this book, the Southern cooks shared their long protected recipes, but it wouldn't be an adventure if everyone

cooperated. Some of these institutions guarded their recipes as though they were members of the family. Thank God, I know how to eat and cook. For the holdouts, I have recreated their dishes, and I'm hoping to get their seal of approval. My mission will be to deliver the most amazing Southern recipes while telling the stories of the people behind the scenes crafting these genuine dishes.

My travels took me to many places, but most importantly, they taught me about the history of the people and places, and the labor of love that is invested into these businesses. My journey writing this book gave me a deeper understanding of how these restaurants stay in business for so many generations. It isn't as much about the profit and loss statement as it is about the relationship and bond that food can create. How many generations are we away from losing the stories of standing at a grandmother's knee to learn how to make biscuits? We are closer than anyone would ever admit. We are losing the traditions that connect our families and prepare our children for their own journeys. But these institutions seem to make preserving those traditions seem effortless.

These owners often talk about putting blood, sweat, and tears into their restaurants, along with a healthy dose of family money. They talk about surviving rough patches, adapting to change, and growing through it. I'm impressed by their stamina. I know the hurdles of operating a profitable restaurant firsthand, and how difficult it can be. There's something awe-inspiring when you're looking into the eyes of someone who has kept his head above water for almost sixty years. Now that's a different kind of restaurateur all together. I know the term for the entrepreneur who opens restaurants is "restaurateur," but shouldn't there be another title for someone who operates a restaurant without classical culinary training, without financial means, without the ability to create a business model? In no way do I suggest this with an ounce of disrespect to the Southern café managers and owners. I merely wonder this out of pure respect and awe. It's amazing and, frankly, so uncommon these days. The steadfastness of these owners in and of itself is worthy of a road trip, just to share the space and a conversation with the folks who make it happen.

Southern hospitality is something of a lost art for my generation. It's a skill that's been practiced for hundreds of years and has defined entire areas of the country. This adventure is certainly Southern-inspired, and that means it will take a little longer than normal because in the South, we take our time in lots of ways, but none more so than at the dinner table or in the kitchen. When I finally convinced my

wife and my publisher that these stories were important to share, I set out for an absolutely life-changing journey that I will never forget. I invite you to read along and discover exactly what it is about authentic Southern food that makes it so special, but more importantly, the stories of the people who have made hospitality their life's work.

The bonding of family over food is a worldwide tradition and still very strongly celebrated in the South. Grandma's sweet potato recipe gets handed down, and family gatherings just aren't the same without it. The meat and three restaurants carry on this tradition of time-tested recipes and family togetherness. The restaurants are usually family-owned, and the regulars are greeted as though they are kinfolk. Kids are welcome, and out-of-town guests are welcomed to the city with some good "home" cooking. It's the consistency of not evolving that provides the romantic allure to visitors and transplants. Don't be in a hurry. It's not a fast stride, but has a steady pace, set out of respect for what might happen and is happening now. There are indescribable forces of sustainability in the mindset of being a Southerner. I'm convinced of these forces of nature as my journey continues.

I've known for some time that the meat and three restaurants have Southern food

figured out. Theirs is a "never skip a step" type of cooking with tasty, authentic recipes. Sometimes I find it even more fascinating how these little country restaurants have taken root in a location that was never intended to be a restaurant—from pharmacies to army bunkers. Its inhabitants took something that was blighted, then rejuvenated the look and feel, and emptied their souls into a building that eventually became an extension of their own homes. The warmth you feel in these places isn't from the decor or the owner's choice of paint color; instead, it exudes from the very people within the place.

"Authentic" is hard to define when talking about Southern food, as at its core it's based on so many cultures and such a varied list of ingredients. It's real, pure, and although there are impostors developing a plan to fancy up or refine America's first true food style, the South has one last line of defense—the Southern meat and three restaurant. I mean someone's grandmother stopped long enough several hundred years ago to note the steps and ingredients it took to create the most delightful flaky piecrust or how to soak and boil black-eyed peas without splitting the skins, and then determined just how much salt to add to the water. These are the types of recipes and the traditions being carried on by the Southern

meat and three restaurants. The labor of love is the food, and in the South it goes deeper than the flour bin. The recipes are handed down like grandpa's pocket watch, an heirloom if you will, handwritten, never altered, and always followed. Family recipes are the Bible of Southern cooking.

My journey has reminded me that food has the power to transport us through space and time to pivotal moments in our lives. I first became a chef to become a part of that—the power of a memory, complete with taste, touch, and smell. The stories behind food are sometimes romantic and personal. Each story you find here is original but somehow vaguely familiar. You believe you may have heard it before, but then you know it's brand new. It begins with what was on the stove, how it smelled, and how it hinted at the secret of

the recipe. It's the same type of story, authentic, somehow loving in its memory. Even if there is a critical tone, you know immediately it's coming from a good place. It's a personal story that allows the storyteller and the listener to remember a life event that was possibly not motivated by food, but was recalled by food. It's a starry-eyed and interesting phenomenon—having a personal story to share with my friends and family, and, especially, my children of times passed, but never forgotten, shared over a hot meal.

Within these pages are not only delicious offerings of homemade, time-tested recipes but also the most important ingredient: the stories of the people and families behind them. May this book remind you that every meal is an occasion for a memory. So sit back, unwind, set your watch to Southern time, and dig in.

ALABAMA

O ne of the best parts about taking this journey and writing this book was rediscovering places that I may have taken for granted. When I think of Alabama, I think of the true Southern slow pace of life. Then I remember that Huntsville was the birthplace of America's space program, that Birmingham owes its almost overnight population growth to the steel industry, and that Mobile was the birthplace of Mardi Gras. Alabama is more than Southern folks allowing time to pass by while sitting in rockers on a country porch. It's made up of people who are inventive, industrious, and know how to have a good time.

As I traveled the state, I was fortunate to run into several souls who fit those descriptions. Being true down-to-earth Southerners, they take great pride in their Southern hospitality, and it shows.

Rebellious by nature, Alabama was the center of the Confederacy during the Civil War, hosting the First White House of the Confederacy. Today, you may think that the war rages on with so many re-enactments taking place across the state. From more recent history, however, Birmingham and Montgomery have several monuments dedicated to the civil rights movement. Alabama is not at war with its past but makes an effort to remind visitors and locals alike of its rich history.

From the airfields of Tuskegee to the oval tracks of Talladega, Alabama has a story to tell around every bend and curve. Its landscape is rich with mountains, piedmont, waterways, and the northwestern shoals. If you've lost a bag on an airline, just stop by Scottsboro, home of the Unclaimed Baggage Center. Who knows? You just may get lucky and find that bag full of clothes that you've lusted after all these years that we both know won't fit you anymore. Or you can just stick to the basics and follow my route to meet some great characters and eat some delicious Southern vittles.

Beans & Greens

Gadsden, Alabama

Some of the best places I've ever eaten are off the beaten path, and Beans & Greens in Gadsden is no different. You don't wander into this place by chance. If you've found this little country restaurant, it's because you're either a local or were nice enough to the locals to have them guide you here. Beans & Greens is an all-wood building with a pine interior, made especially for country folk.

Bobby Boles, the current owner, started his career in the place as a dishwasher. When the previous owner fell upon bad health, he handed the restaurant over to Bobby, and with his wife, Kelly, he's been running it for more than a decade. The restaurant is buffet style but sometimes offers special menus. The regulars tend to prefer the fourteen to eighteen items on the buffet with the salad bar that includes coleslaw and potato salad.

The restaurant is often busy, but customers usually don't have to wait long for a table since there is a fairly quick turn-around time with the buffet service. The staff is very friendly, and Bobby isn't afraid to get in the mix when the place fills up. There is usually a selection of five or six meats with choices such as chicken fingers, roast beef, meatloaf, and chicken and dressing. Then come the veggies— corn, baked beans, green beans, sweet potato casserole, and macaroni and cheese.

There was no special menu the day I was guided to Beans & Greens, so I went for the buffet. Everything looked amazing, so I sampled nearly everything on the line. I was careful, though, to save room for dessert. My sources had told me that the made-from-scratch sweet treats were not to be missed.

I felt pretty full already, so I went for a slightly lighter dessert option: the strawberry shortcake. In the South, when strawberries are in season, this delicious, light and fluffy confection makes an appearance at most outdoor parties. To celebrate the summer fruit harvest, places such as Castleberry (northeast of Montgomery) and Loxely in Baldwin County host strawberry festivals. And after a couple of bites of the strawberry shortcake at Beans & Greens, I can see what all the hoopla is about.

The shortcake is sweet, moist, light, and airy. The fresh ripe strawberries are bathed in the perfect simple syrup to complement the cake, and a dollop of whipped cream tops the whole thing off. It was the ideal ending to my meal, and I decided right then and there to perfect that recipe myself. So feel free to recreate this delicious treat at home, and don't hesitate to ask the locals in Gadsden for directions to Beans & Greens to try the original.

Strawberry Shortcake (page 4)

STRAWBERRY SHORTCAKE

1 (16-ounce) box yellow cake mix

4 large eggs

1/3 cup vegetable oil

1 cup sugar, divided

3 pints strawberries, sliced

3 cups heavy cream

Preheat the oven to 350 degrees. Grease two 9-inch baking pans.

In a large bowl combine the cake mix, eggs, and oil, along with the amount of water called for on the box. Beat until well incorporated. Divide the batter between the two pans. Bake for 30 minutes, or until a wooden pick inserted near the center comes out clean. Let the cakes cool for 15 minutes on a wire rack before removing them from the pans. Let cool completely on a wire rack before assembling.

Sprinkle 1/2 cup of the sugar over the strawberries. Set aside at room temperature until the berries release their juices, about 30 minutes.

Combine the heavy cream and the remaining 1/2 cup sugar in a medium bowl, and whip by hand or with a hand mixer until stiff peaks form. Place one of the cake layers on a serving platter. Add half the strawberries and half the whipped cream. Top with the second cake layer and the remaining whipped cream. Place the remaining strawberries on the top.

Serves 8.

Charles' Cafeteria & Grill

Fayette, Alabama

n 1985 Charles Langley opened Charles' Cafeteria & Grill to serve the community of Fayette and the surrounding areas. He saw a need for a local restaurant that offered fresh local meats, produce, and homemade desserts, without breaking the bank for the local folk. After a while, Charles retired, leaving his daughter, Belinda, and her husband, Mike Watts, to run the business. I always love to hear about how businesses got started and, even better, how they have stayed in the family.

Whatever values Charles instilled in Belinda and Mike are still going strong today. The place is very busy, but the staff is extremely accommodating to guests and very friendly. There was a certain hum of energy when I walked in the door, with all the staff rushing around to greet hungry customers, not in a "get out of my way" kind of vibe, but in a nice and energetic way.

This place has a great breakfast menu with made-from-scratch biscuits daily. There's a daily lunch buffet with meats and a choice of several different fresh and seasonal veggies. The thing that really piqued my interest, though, was the desserts. I have a lot of respect for restaurants that make their own desserts daily. As a chef, I know the time it takes

to make that kind of commitment to your customers. It is truly a labor of love. I got my plate and headed to the buffet, but the whole time, my mind focused on dessert. The food from the buffet was great, but I couldn't wait to taste a fresh homemade sweet treat.

I happened upon Charles' Cafeteria & Grill in the Alabama summer, when the heat is somewhat unbearable, especially if you grew up in a cooler climate and aren't used to it. That being said, it was the perfect time to partake in the restaurant's strawberry pie. I knew the fruit would be ripe and delicious and the perfect antidote to the sweltering summer heat.

When the pie arrived at my table, I knew I had made a wise choice. The beautiful color of the strawberries let me know that I was going to enjoy every bite. The crust was light and delicate, and the filling was just sweet enough not to overwhelm the fruit. It was the perfect summer pie.

The next time you are looking for a light dessert that captures the essence of a Southern summer, just use the recipe I've included on the next page. It's a great after-dinner treat or complement to any outdoor picnic. If you ever happen to be in Fayette in the midst of summer, don't hesitate to drop by Charles' Cafeteria & Grill for the real thing.

Piecrust

1 ½ cups all-purpose flour, divided

2 tablespoons sugar

½ teaspoon salt

6 tablespoons cold butter

¼ cup vegetable shortening

½ cup ice water

Filling

4 pints fresh strawberries, divided

1 cup sugar

2 tablespoons cornstarch

Pinch of salt

1 tablespoon lemon juice

STRAWBERRY PIE

For the crust, place ¾ cup of the flour, sugar, and salt in the bowl of a food processor and pulse until mixed well. Add the butter and shortening and process until the dough just starts to clump together. Scrape the sides and bottom of the bowl with a rubber spatula and redistribute the dough around the processor blade. Add ½ cup flour and pulse until the mixture is evenly distributed. Add the ice water one tablespoon at a time until the mixture forms a ball. Transfer the mixture to a medium bowl.

Place a piece of plastic wrap on a work surface and place the dough on top. Flatten the dough into a 4-inch disk. Wrap in plastic wrap and refrigerate for at least 1 hour.

Preheat the oven to 425 degrees.

Dust a work surface with the remaining ¼ cup flour. Remove the dough from the refrigerator and unwrap. Place it on the work surface. Roll the dough into a 12-inch circle about ⅛ inch thick. Place the dough in a pie pan, leaving the overhanging dough in place, and refrigerate until the dough is firm, about 30 minutes.

Remove the pan from the refrigerator. Fold the overhanging dough under and flute the edges or press the tines of a fork against the dough to flatten it against the rim of the pie pan. Refrigerate until firm.

Remove the pie pan from the refrigerator and use a fork to prick the bottom of the dough. Line the crust with foil and fill with pie weights or dried beans. Bake for 15 minutes. Remove the foil and weights. Rotate the pan and bake for an additional 5 to 10 minutes, until the crust is golden-brown and crisp. Let cool to room temperature.

For the filling, pour 2 pints of the berries into the bowl of a food processor and process until smooth, 20 to 30 seconds, scraping down the bowl as needed.

Whisk the sugar, cornstarch, and salt in a medium saucepan. Stir in the berry puree. Cook over high heat, stirring constantly, and bring to a full boil. Transfer the mixture to a large bowl and stir in the lemon juice. Let cool to room temperature.

Add the remaining 2 pints berries to the bowl with the glaze and fold gently with a rubber spatula until the berries are evenly coated. Scoop the berries into the piecrust, piling into a mound. Refrigerate the pie until chilled, about 5 hours for a perfectly firm pie.

Serves 8.

Clara's Country Café

Clanton, Alabama

No matter what part of the country you are from, I can guarantee that in every city or town there is a place that plays into the local sports rivalries. In Clanton, Clara's Country Café likes to bring warring rivals together to eat under the same roof. Even Auburn and Alabama fans agree that the food at Clara's is a touchdown.

Like many of the great establishments I've visited on my journey through the South, Clara's is a little off the beaten path of Interstate 65, but worth the slight detour. The exterior of the building, with its stone walls and a slatted sign over the door, made me think more of an upscale steakhouse than a country buffet. But once I stepped inside, the smells and small clusters of tables told me that I wasn't lost.

The buffet isn't sprawling, usually offering a couple of entrées and a handful of veggies to choose from. But what Clara's may lack in quantity, it makes up for in quality. The limited offerings allow Clara's to provide everything fresh and hot to its customers. It must be working, because they keep coming back. And when I asked locals about a good place to grab some home cooking, they all replied with the name Clara's.

The day I happened upon Clara's, the featured entrées were fried chicken and Salisbury steak. The veggies included black-eyed peas, French fries, green beans, greens, and creamed potatoes. I knew that I couldn't go wrong, and with everything looking so amazing, I sampled some of everything. The chicken was crispy without being greasy, and the Salisbury steak brought back a cozy TV dinner feeling to my tummy.

The veggies weren't slackers either. With the right amount of tenderness to complement their earthy flavor, the black-eyed peas weren't overcooked. The greens were tender and well-seasoned. But the standout of the buffet that day, for me, was the creamed potatoes. That's no false advertising. I'm sure there was enough butter and cream in those potatoes to support the local dairy farmers, but all I was thinking about was how good they tasted going down. The texture was amazing—so smooth with just the right amount of salt. I made it my mission to recreate this silky side and hope that the recipe below does it justice. If not, feel free to stop by Clara's Country Café the next time you are passing through Clanton and need a little break from the monotony of the drive on I-65.

CREAMED POTATOES

5 russet potatoes, peeled and cut into cubes

1 tablespoon salt, plus more to taste

6 tablespoons butter

1 tablespoon flour

2/3 to 1 cup whole milk

Freshly cracked black pepper to taste

Place the cubed potatoes in a medium saucepan and cover with cold water. Add 1 tablespoon of the salt. Bring the water to a boil over high heat. Reduce the heat to medium and cook until the potatoes are just done, 6 to 8 minutes.

Pour off all but about 1/2 cup of the cooking liquid. Return the pan to the heat, add the butter, and stir until melted. Gradually add the flour, stirring until well incorporated. Add 2/3 cup of the milk and stir well. Add a generous grinding of pepper and taste. Add additional milk and salt if necessary. The potatoes should be slightly lumpy but fully cooked, with a creamy consistency.

Serves 6.

Cock of the Walk

Opelika, Alabama

Every region has its own traditional sayings, and if you're not from that area, they usually sound pretty strange and don't make much sense. In Opelika a group of folks used one such saying as the name of their restaurant, the Cock of the Walk. According to the owners, the saying means the best of the best. The first restaurant opened in 1977 as a catfish house in Natchez, Mississippi, but with the growing support of customers, the owners soon expanded the menu and locations, including the one I visited in Opelika.

The dining room's wooden tables, wooden slat chairs, and simple decor give the building a very rustic feel. Because the restaurant is situated on a lake, guests flow out to the back dock to feed the fish and turtles and admire the beautiful strutting peacocks on site. It's a very picturesque little place to enjoy a good home-cooked meal.

It's also entertaining. The staff flips the skillet jalapeño cornbread in the dining room so high it seems to go over the rafters, but they're careful not to knock into any of the fine examples of taxidermy lining the walls.

The food is served in tin plates with tin cups to drink from. It kind of made me want to pull out my sleeping bag and try to earn my wilderness badge, but then I remembered that I'm no Boy Scout. The menu has a variety of fried fish, shellfish, pork chops, and chicken tenders, or if you prefer, you can have the same protein grilled. They also have a selection of po' boy sandwiches and salads.

I went for the fried flounder with cheese grits, coleslaw, skillet cornbread, and pickled onions. The portions were huge, and everything tasted so good that I wished I could expand my stomach to eat a few more bites. The fish was nice and crispy with a mild, light flavor and good seasoning in the breading. The pickled onions were a nice, tart treat to accompany the richness of the cheese grits. Surprisingly, though, the best thing on my plate was the creamy coleslaw.

In the South, coleslaw is a must-have at any picnic or backyard barbecue. I often overlook it as a side, but at the Cock of the Walk, the coleslaw commanded my attention. How can I not share the recipe with you for something that is so simple and delicious and can add enjoyment to your next outdoor get together? And the next time you feel the call of the wild, make a trip to the Cock of the Walk in Opelika and fill up before you wrestle that bear.

COLESLAW

1 cup mayonnaise

3 tablespoons sugar

2 tablespoons cider vinegar

½ cup vegetable oil

⅛ teaspoon onion powder

¼ teaspoon celery salt

¼ teaspoon freshly cracked black pepper

¼ teaspoon salt

1 tablespoon lemon juice

1 large head cabbage, finely shredded

2 large carrots, finely shredded

In a large bowl combine the mayonnaise, sugar, vinegar, and oil. Add the onion powder, celery salt, pepper, and salt. Whisk in the lemon juice until well blended. Toss the shredded cabbage and carrots with the dressing until they are well coated. Refrigerate for 30 minutes or until ready to serve.

Serves 8 to 10.

Pannie-George's Kitchen

Auburn, Alabama

When you walk into Pannie-George's Kitchen in Auburn, you feel as though you are being welcomed into the family. In 2005 the family of Mary (Pannie) and George Taylor set out to accomplish two simple goals: to serve their community and to get more people to taste their family's food. Pannie-George is a combination of their names, and their restaurant is designed to expand the traditions they created. When they first started, they hosted the family and whatever friends and neighbors came along for supper after church. Their children decided to expand the reach of this Sunday supper to the community seven days a week.

Guests are served cafeteria-style in this family-run joint, and I do mean family-run. Pannie and George's children and grandchildren run the place. They welcome you like family and make sure that you get a healthy helping of Southern hospitality to go along with your other selections. Customers walk along the cafeteria line and make food choices before paying the cashier and snagging their tray at the end of the line.

As I scanned the offerings of the day, I knew I had my work cut out for me. I saw the fried chicken offered daily due to its popularity and plenty of other entrées, including beef tips, country-fried steak,

and pork chops. And don't even get me started on the sides. The offerings were a Southern vegetable daydream with everything from green beans to corn casserole to black-eyed peas and, according to customers, some of the best mac 'n' cheese within thirty miles.

I settled on the fried chicken as my entrée and chose the black-eyed peas, green beans, and broccoli, rice, and cheese casserole to complement my plate. As I headed to my table with my tray, I wasn't even the slightest bit worried that I had made the wrong choice, because from where I was sitting, there was no such thing. The fried chicken was crispy and slightly salty, but in the good, Southern way. The green beans and black-eyed peas were seasoned and cooked well, but the real star of the show, for me, was the broccoli, rice, and cheese casserole.

Broccoli is one of those veggies that you usually have to coerce your kids into eating. But when it's tossed with rice and encased in cheese, parents have no such problem. The result is a tasty and satisfying side that makes you feel all warm inside. Use the following recipe to convince your kids that broccoli can be delicious, or just to remind yourself. And the next time you're in Auburn, be sure to stop in and sample the tasty goodies at Pannie-George's Kitchen for yourself.

3 cups broccoli florets, cut into bite-size pieces

1 (10-ounce) can condensed cream of chicken soup

3 cups cooked rice (white or brown)

1 ¾ cups shredded Cheddar cheese

½ cup mayonnaise

1 teaspoon kosher salt

1 teaspoon vinegar-based hot sauce

¾ cup crushed corn flakes

2 tablespoons butter, melted

BROCCOLI, RICE, AND CHEESE CASSEROLE

Preheat the oven to 375 degrees. Grease a 9 x 9-inch baking dish. Combine the broccoli, soup, rice, cheese, mayonnaise, salt, and hot sauce in a large bowl. Fold gently with a spatula to combine. Do not stir. Pour the mixture into the prepared pan. Sprinkle the crushed corn flakes over the top and drizzle evenly with the butter.

Bake uncovered for 30 minutes, until hot through the center and golden brown on the top. Let stand for 10 minutes before serving.

Serves 6 to 8.

Red's Little School House

Grady, Alabama

Have you ever wondered what it must have been like in the old days when your schoolhouse was a single room with all ages mixed in together and some "school marm" up in front with a ruler in her hand? Well, you may have some *Little House on the Prairie* flashbacks when you walk into Red's Little School House in Grady. It's exactly what you are imagining from the name—a small red wooden building with a black roof. Inside are nostalgic touches including old wooden sleds on the wall and a chalkboard with a map of the continents.

But this schoolhouse isn't in the business of educating youngsters anymore. No sir, nowadays this little schoolhouse is in the business of feeding people delicious home-cooked Southern food and expanding belt lines. Built in 1910, Red's became a restaurant in 1985. Customers may eat from a buffet or order off of the menu. The day I made it to Red's Little School House, I was famished, and the buffet looked so amazing that I decided, for once, to forgo the menu and dive right into the buffet.

The buffet included, among other things, fried chicken and pulled pork barbecue with a hodgepodge of veggies, including baked beans, squash casserole, green beans, and apple and cheese casserole. I piled my plate high with whatever I could carry, knowing I would pay the price for my indulgence later, but telling myself all the while not to worry my pretty little head about that. I sat down and dug in, and I must say I got a lesson in the School House that day—a lesson about how to clean my plate.

I savored every bite. The apple and cheese casserole was a new one for me but very tasty, indeed. Everything hit the spot, but my favorite dish of the day had to be the pulled pork barbecue. Every region has its own twist on barbecue, especially in the South. This pork was cooked low and slow, for sure, with plenty of moisture left in the meat and the flavor of smoke that made my taste buds do a happy dance. The baked beans were a great complement, and the fried cornbread was just the icing on the cake for the meal.

I don't pretend to be a barbecue guru, but if you follow this recipe, you too can experience the joy that only pulled pork can bring. Don't be afraid to educate yourself to the merits of the age-old tradition of barbecue. When you happen to find yourself in Grady, make sure you stop by Red's Little School House for some culinary education on the subject of tastiness.

BARBECUED PULLED PORK SANDWICHES

Place the pork in a 6-quart slow cooker.

In a small bowl mix the ketchup, brown sugar, vinegar, salt, paprika, pepper, onion powder, and garlic powder until smooth and creamy. Pour over the pork. Cover the slow cooker and cook for 6 to 7 hours on low. Remove the pork from the slow cooker and let it cool.

When the pork has cooled enough to handle, shred it using two forks and then return it to the slow cooker juices. Mix and allow the sauce to permeate the shredded meat. Serve on hamburger buns.

Serves 8 to 10.

3 pounds pork shoulder, trimmed

1 cup ketchup

1 cup packed light brown sugar

½ cup cider vinegar

4 tablespoons kosher salt

¼ cup smoked paprika

3 tablespoons freshly cracked black pepper

1 teaspoon onion powder

1 teaspoon garlic powder

Hamburger buns for serving

Sisters' Restaurant

Troy, Alabama

When I walked into Sisters' Restaurant in Troy, I was surprised by the size of the place. It was warm and welcoming with a large open dining room and smiling servers. The owners are, as you would assume, sisters. Geraldine Umbehagen and Pat Rogers have run the place for more than a decade now and enjoy sharing their love of Southern cooking with others. When you ask the residents of Troy about a good place to find some home cooking, they all will point you in the direction of Sisters' Restaurant.

It's not often that you find a restaurant that rightfully claims to be the best place to be on both a Friday night and Sunday after church. With its Friday night seafood buffet and Sunday country buffet, Sisters' fills the needs for both. I wandered in on a Tuesday, and although there wasn't a buffet, the menu seemed plentiful.

I was in need of some comfort food, and it looked as though I was in the right place. There was plenty to choose from, but I went for the meatloaf with mashed potatoes, fried okra, and string beans. I had heard that the banana pudding was the stuff of legends, so I ordered that for dessert as well. My meal was great and made me feel very comforted, but I was looking forward to my sweet treat dessert.

Banana pudding is something of a Southern staple. It's usually a mixture of banana pudding, fresh bananas, and vanilla wafers and can be topped with whipped cream or served alone. Every Southern cook has a bevy of little touches that he or she adds to make the pudding a signature dish, and Sisters' Restaurant is no different.

When my pudding arrived, I knew I was going to enjoy it. Sisters' serves banana pudding in a sundae dish, immediately signaling that sugar is on its way. The pudding was amazing, sweet and creamy with just the right mix of vanilla wafers and fresh bananas to add texture. I unashamedly licked my bowl clean and promised myself that I would share this sweet goodness with my children.

On the next page I've listed a recipe for banana pudding that is both simple and delicious. Desserts can get so complicated sometimes, but this one is easy to make and guaranteed to be a crowd pleaser. The next time you happen to pass through Troy, stop by Sisters' Restaurant to try the original for yourself.

1 (12-ounce) box vanilla wafers

1 ½ cups sugar

½ cup all-purpose flour

1 teaspoon salt

5 large egg yolks

2 ½ cups milk

1 teaspoon vanilla extract

1 tablespoon butter

6 ripe bananas

Meringue

4 large egg whites, at room temperature

¼ teaspoon cream of tartar

7 tablespoons sugar

1 teaspoon vanilla extract

BANANA PUDDING

Preheat the oven to 375 degrees.

For the banana pudding, line the bottom of a 9-inch square baking dish with a layer of vanilla wafers.

Combine the sugar, flour, and salt in a medium bowl and mix well.

Place the egg yolks in a heavy saucepan and beat with a whisk over medium heat. Add the sugar mixture and cook until the sugar dissolves, stirring constantly. Add the milk and vanilla and bring to a boil. When the mixture begins to thicken add the butter. Remove the pan from the heat.

Peel the bananas and slice into ½-inch rounds. Place a layer of the slices in the baking dish on top of the vanilla wafers. Pour half of the pudding over the banana layer. Add another layer of vanilla wafers and another layer of banana slices, and cover with the remaining pudding.

For the meringue, beat the egg whites with a hand mixer until soft peaks form. Add the cream of tartar and gradually add the sugar, 1 tablespoon at a time, while beating. Fold the vanilla into the meringue and then spread it over the pudding.

Bake until the meringue is brown, for 10 to 12 minutes.

Let cool slightly, then chill in the refrigerator for at least 2 hours. The pudding is best if chilled overnight.

Serves 10.

Swamp John's

Red Bay, Alabama

love to hear the stories from owners of places busting at the seams due to the good food being served and the expansions that followed. I encountered one of the most unique of such stories as I talked to the owner of Swamp John's in Red Bay. The restaurant started as a mobile catering business fashioned from an old grocery store truck. John Shewbart, the culinary mastermind behind Swamp John's, traveled around and hosted fish frys. Eventually, he set up shop in a small former gas station in Red Bay.

As his fish fries grew more popular, John gained some support from investors and procured a small forty-seat restaurant in Muscle Shoals, complete with drive-through service. Swamp John's has been busy from the start, and it doesn't seem to be slowing down. The new restaurant's decor is not what you might expect from a guy who got his start in an old grocery store truck. The look is very clean and modern with bright reds and blues on the walls and bright lime-green vinyl tablecloths, complete with modern metal chairs.

But the original location in Red Bay is quite a different story. The gas pumps stand watch in front of the restaurant, and the outside seating is simple heavy-duty picnic tables. The food is served on Styrofoam plates with plastic cutlery. The building looks like a place where you might buy bait if you are going to catch a catfish, not a place you would sit down to eat one. If you're looking for ambiance, you may want to make the trip to Muscle Shoals, but if you're looking for a good meal, wander no farther than Red Bay.

The menu is what you would expect at a joint called Swamp John's—heavy on the seafood with some chicken and po' boys thrown in for good measure. Customers may choose a plate lunch with an entrée, two sides, hushpuppies, onion (a traditional accoutrement for fried catfish in the South), and a pickle. With John's huge following for his fried catfish, I decided to see what all the fuss was about.

I got the large plate, which has four catfish fillets, sweet potato fries, and coleslaw. The fish and fries were fresh out of the fryer, and the catfish was a beautiful golden brown. I almost forgot that I was sitting in a gas station. The breading was seasoned well and very crispy, and the fish was light, flaky, and obviously fresh. I ate all four of my fillets and didn't even leave a crumb.

Hopefully the following recipe can provide you with a modicum of the pleasure I experienced that day at Swamp John's in Red Bay. If not, you can always make the trip down South. Who knows, maybe you will get lucky and catch the old mobile kitchen at a local supermarket for a fundraiser. If not, you can always sample the goodies at the Muscle Shoals location.

FRIED CATFISH

Pour 2 inches of vegetable oil into a deep skillet and heat over medium-high. Place a wire rack in a baking sheet lined with paper towels.

Place the catfish fillets in a single layer in a shallow dish and cover with milk. In a large bowl combine the cornmeal, salt, pepper, paprika, onion powder, and garlic powder.

Remove the catfish from the milk and sprinkle with salt and pepper. Dredge the catfish in the cornmeal mixture and press firmly on both sides, and then shake off the excess.

When the oil reaches 350 degrees, add one or two fillets, and fry until golden brown, about 4 minutes on each side. Transfer the catfish to the wire rack while you prepare the remaining fish. Serve immediately.

Serves 6.

Vegetable oil for frying

6 (4- to 5-ounce) catfish fillets

2 ½ cups whole milk

3 cups yellow cornmeal

2 ½ tablespoons kosher salt, plus more for sprinkling

2 teaspoons freshly cracked black pepper, plus more for sprinkling

1 teaspoon paprika

1 teaspoon onion powder

1 teaspoon garlic powder

Victoria's Restaurant

Jasper, Alabama

I wasn't sure I was in the right place when I walked into Victoria's Restaurant in Jasper. Women's clothing and all sorts of handbags, accessories, and Alabama sports paraphernalia surrounded me. As it turns out, Victoria's is a restaurant, gift shop, and boutique. I was quickly corralled to the right part of the establishment, and from there on out, I was no longer confused. The rows of delicious baked goods, including cupcakes, pies, and cakes, reassured me that women's apparel wasn't the owner's only passion.

Established in 1993, Victoria's is a family-owned restaurant cooking up old-fashioned Southern favorites for locals and travelers alike. According to the sign outside, it's "where good food and good friends come together." The small, white building has a small, open dining room with minimal frivolities, except for the very inviting deli case full of desserts. The owner, Kerry Boyd, is very friendly and loves to get feedback from her customers. The locals guided me here when I asked where I could get a good meal.

The smells from the kitchen were delicious and as I looked over the menu, I was happy I had followed their advice. The day I wandered in, Victoria's was serving a variety of meats and veggies, as usual. After a bit of deliberation, I settled on the meatloaf, candied yams, purple hull peas, and fried okra. My meal arrived, and every last bite was something worth writing home about. I couldn't wait to sample the delicious desserts I had passed on my way in.

The choice was harder because everything looked like a winner. I selected the peanut butter pie, and when it arrived at my table, the first bite let me know everything I needed to know. The crust was graham cracker, adding the perfect texture and sweetness to the rich, creamy, decadent pie. The filling itself was amazing, creamy and smooth with the perfect flavor of peanut butter that didn't overpower.

I scooped up every last crumb of the pie and left feeling very satisfied and possibly a few pounds heavier. After several attempts, I finally was able to recreate that delectable peanut butter pie in my own kitchen, and being the very benevolent man that I am, I have decided to share its goodness with you. But the next time you happen to be in Jasper, pop into Victoria's Restaurant and pick up a slice of heaven for yourself and maybe even a new purse.

PEANUT BUTTER PIE

Preheat the oven to 350 degrees.

In a medium bowl mix the graham cracker crumbs and butter. Press the mixture into the bottom and up the sides of an ungreased 9-inch pie plate. Bake for 8 minutes, or until the crust is lightly browned. Let cool.

In a medium bowl whisk the milk and pudding mix. In another medium bowl beat the peanut butter, cream cheese, and condensed milk with a hand mixer on medium speed until smooth and creamy.

Pour the melted chocolate onto the bottom of the piecrust.

In a large bowl whip the heavy cream until it begins to thicken and then add the sugar. Fold 2 cups of the whipped cream into the pudding mixture and pour it into the crust. Spread the remaining whipped cream over top and refrigerate the pie for at least 2 hours before serving.

Serves 8.

3 cups crushed graham crackers

1/3 cup butter, melted

2 cups milk

1 (3-ounce) package instant vanilla pudding mix

1 cup creamy peanut butter

6 ounces cream cheese, softened

1 cup sweetened condensed milk

1/2 cup chocolate chips, melted

1 cup heavy cream

2 tablespoons sugar

ARKANSAS

When you travel west across the state of Arkansas from the Mississippi River, it isn't hard to see that agriculture is king. Miles and miles of flat, open farmland stretch all the way from the river to the capital of Little Rock. It's no surprise to find some delicious meat and three restaurants in the state that leads the country in the production of catfish, turkeys, eggs, soybeans, pecans, and rice. And that's not even the entire list.

It's hard for me to believe when I drive through this part of the state that Arkansas is actually home to two mountain ranges, the Ozarks and the Ouachita. People here love the outdoors and are big proponents of hunting, fishing, camping, and hiking. That would definitely explain how the state got its nickname, "The Natural State."

Arkansas natives are also huge fans of football. Don't even get them started talking about football unless you are fully prepared for the repercussions. I never thought that a pig call could bring a group of people together until I traveled through this state and heard, more times than I could count, someone cry out "Woo! Pig Sooie!" It took me a while to realize that someone's pig had not escaped and that, instead, a football game was on. The University of Arkansas holds the official trademark of the call now, believe it or not.

Arkansas has seen its share of tumultuous times, during both the Civil War and the civil rights movement. In 1957, nine African American students made national headlines when they braved a hostile crowd to integrate the Little Rock Central High School, only to be removed by police later for their own safety. But this first step was integral to carrying out the Supreme Court's decision to integrate educational institutions in the groundbreaking *Brown v. Board of Education of Topeka*.

With famous natives such as Bill Clinton, Johnny Cash, and John Grisham, the state isn't known for people who keep their opinions or thoughts to themselves, and honestly that seems to have worked out well so far. Arkansans have a strong spirit and lots of personality, to say the least, and there was

no shortage of either with the characters I met during my edible journey across this state. From the humble and generous husband and wife team of Sean and Jackie Sikes at the Greater Good Café to the sweet little retired-but-not-retired Sue Robinson Williams at Sue's Kitchen, the people of Arkansas were genuine in their character, welcoming, and ready to make sure I didn't leave hungry.

So if you're feeling cooped up and need some fresh outdoor air, don't hesitate to travel to Arkansas. The locals will be happy to show you the best fishing spot or the prettiest view or even the best local place to get a good meal. And if you follow my guide, you won't leave the state hungry or let down.

Calico County

Fort Smith, Arkansas

When you sit down at a table in Calico County restaurant in Fort Smith, you might get the feeling right off the bat that the staff is trying to sweeten you up. Unlike most restaurants where servers greet you with a basket of hot rolls, the staff at Calico County suck you right in with deliciously sweet and gooey cinnamon rolls. The atmosphere has a small town feel, even though Fort Smith is the second largest city in the state. Wood paneling on the walls and older lighting fixtures give the place a dull glow. There's even a sign to the restrooms that mentions pay phones. Do those still exist?

The cinnamon rolls are not the only sweetness you get from this place; the staff is also very kind and friendly. As I looked over the menu, I was amused by the fact that despite its appearance, this place must be keeping up with the times since they offer both a "traditional" portion and a "seniors or lite eaters" portion. Since I'd been pretty consistently overindulging on my journey, I decided to go for the lighter option. I also noticed that I could add soup or salad and a fruit cobbler à la mode, which cemented the deal for my portion size choice. I had to save room for dessert.

All the dishes on the menu looked great, but I was a little homesick and road weary that day, so I selected Mother's Juicy Pot Roast. What says home more than a pot roast? I topped it off with green beans and the sweet potato casserole. Every bite of my dinner was delicious, and I started to question if I made the wrong choice with the portion size.

But then I was greeted with my treat—a bowl of warm peach cobbler with a scoop of vanilla ice cream gently melting over the top. My mouth was watering before the dish even hit the table. With my first bite, I was extremely glad I saved room for this. The peaches were perfect—sweet but not overbearingly so and cooked to just the right texture. The top of the cobbler was a delicious crumble of sweetness that helped to pick up on the hints of tartness in the peaches.

I often forget when making desserts that sometimes the best ones are simple, without a ton of ingredients. Enjoy this simple recipe with family and friends, and don't forget the vanilla ice cream for a true Southern tradition. When you drive into Fort Smith, be sure to stop by Calico County for a taste of the original. You won't be disappointed.

PEACH COBBLER

Preheat the oven to 350 degrees. Grease a 9 x 9-inch square baking dish.

In a large bowl combine the peaches with ¼ cup of the sugar, 2 tablespoons of the flour, vanilla, and lemon peel. Transfer to the baking dish.

In another large bowl combine the remaining ¾ cup sugar, the remaining 1 cup and 6 tablespoons flour, butter, baking powder, and salt. Use a fork to scrape the ingredients together until crumbly. Add the cream and mix until a loose dough ball forms. Drop the dough by spoonsful over the peaches. Avoid covering the entire top, as the dough will come together in the cooking process.

Place the pan on a baking sheet and bake 45 to 55 minutes, until golden brown and bubbly.

Let stand for 10 to 15 minutes before serving to allow the sugary peach syrup to redistribute.

Serves 8.

8 peaches, cut into ½-inch thick wedges

1 cup sugar, divided

1 ½ cups all-purpose flour, divided

1 teaspoon vanilla extract

1 teaspoon finely grated fresh lemon peel

6 tablespoons butter, cubed and chilled

1 teaspoon baking powder

¼ teaspoon salt

1 cup heavy cream

Greater Good Café

Clinton, Arkansas

Sean and Jackie Sikes aren't your typical restaurant owners. While profit margins are on the forefront of most restaurant owners' minds, Sean and Jackie buck that system completely. At the Greater Good Café in Clinton, patrons are asked to pay only what they can afford. For those with heftier pocketbooks, it's recommended that they pay it forward by being more generous with the amount. The couple wants to be sure that everyone gets enough to eat, regardless of their ability to pay.

The couple originally started the Dirty Farmers Community Market to provide a place for local farmers to sell their goods and crafts five days a week. Jackie began cooking for customers, and from there, the café was born. Unfortunately, after a car crashed through the storefront, the couple was forced to move the restaurant. Now located on Main Street, the café has played a big role in revitalizing the older downtown area of Clinton.

It seems that wherever this couple goes, good is sure to follow. The café is tiny—just a handful of tables peppered among the wares of the farmers and craftsmen. The atmosphere is very warm and cozy. Jackie is the only cook, and the kitchen is not commercial grade, but she does a great job of feeding a lot of people. Volunteers help serve the guests, and the place actually runs fairly smoothly. Maybe it's the goodwill that everyone shares and knowing that this place is really about something so much more than a good place to eat.

Jackie cooks up something different every day. This restaurant may not totally fit the mold of the other meat and three restaurants I've visited, since there isn't a long list of entrées and sides to choose from, but the determination of the owners to build the community they live in makes this place a must-see for my journey. The daily offerings vary from homemade spaghetti to sweet potato chili to grilled cheese and tomato basil soup. On the day I wandered in, breakfast must have been on Jackie's mind. She was offering up a delicious baked egg and cheese casserole.

I ordered and sat at one of the few tables. The atmosphere was great—the people were very welcoming, and I felt like anything but an outsider. When my plate arrived, I could smell the bacon and couldn't wait to dig in. I happily gobbled up every last bite. At the checkout I paid for my food and purchased a voucher so that if someone who came behind me couldn't pay, they could still eat. Good food and good deeds are meant to be shared. Keep that in mind when you recreate this recipe in your kitchen. And if you happen to be passing through Clinton anytime soon, be sure to stop in and see what Jackie is cooking up, and don't forget to pay it forward if you can.

8 large eggs, at room
temperature

1 cup heavy cream

1 teaspoon kosher salt

2 ounces Gruyère cheese,
shredded

2 ounces white Cheddar
cheese, shredded

2 ounces Brie cheese, cut
into ½ inch pieces

1 bunch green onions, sliced

1 large tomato, thickly sliced

BAKED EGG AND CHEESE CASSEROLE

Preheat the oven to 350 degrees. Grease a 9 x 13-inch casserole dish.

In a large bowl whisk together the eggs, cream, and salt. Pour the mixture into the pan. Sprinkle the cheeses on top and stir them around with a fork. Bake for 30 minutes. Let stand for 15 minutes before serving. Serve with the green onions, a tomato slice, and your favorite breakfast meat.*

Serves 12.

*Jackie suggests serving crisp pieces of pork belly.

JJ's Lakeside Café

Lake Village, Arkansas

Bigger is better when it comes to the food at JJ's Lakeside Café in Lake Village. Maybe it's the hungry customers who wander in from a day of fun in the sun at Lake Chicot that prompted this restaurant into serving plate-size burgers. Or maybe it's just that the owners like to make sure that their customers don't leave hungry. Whatever the reason, you'd better bring your appetite with you when you come to JJ's.

When you walk in, you are greeted by a handful of booths against the wall and some large picnic-style tables in the center of the dining room, complete with the vinyl red-and-white checkered tablecloths. The staff is friendly and fast, two qualities that most endear restaurant workers to me. I was quickly welcomed and handed a menu.

Nestled alongside Lake Chicot, well-known for its largemouth bass population, Lake Village is a great place to try the local fish, and JJ's serves it up by the heaping plateful. That explains why I felt as though fishermen surrounded me. With a place this close to freshwater, I had to try the local fare, and as I looked over the menu I saw that I had plenty to choose from.

I decided to go big or go home and ordered the seafood sampler, which consisted of three frog legs, one stuffed crab, six breaded oysters, a dozen fried shrimp, and three pieces of fried catfish, complete with hushpuppies and coleslaw, of course. When my plate arrived, I knew that my eyes were at least twice as big as my stomach, but I felt it was my duty to at least sample everything on the plate. The breading was crispy with a perfect mix of salt and pepper.

As I got to the frog legs, I knew I was going to be pleasantly surprised. For those of you who haven't had the luxury of tasting them, the rumor is true: they really do taste like chicken—elegant swamp chicken. That might sound unappealing, but they are actually pretty good. It takes a good cook to handle frog legs well, keeping them moist inside while providing a nice crunch to the coating. These bad boys were gone in a matter of minutes, and while everything on the plate was tasty, I have to say that the frog legs stole the show.

So to help you overcome your fears of cooking and eating frog legs, I've included an unbeatable recipe. Maybe trying them at home will help you learn to enjoy this tasty treat. Then the next time you are in Lake Village, you can order them at JJ's Lakeside Café with confidence, knowing you won't be disappointed.

Marinade and Frog Legs

1 large egg

1 cup milk

½ teaspoon garlic powder

1 teaspoon onion powder

2 teaspoons hot sauce

1 teaspoon kosher salt

Freshly cracked black pepper to taste

24 to 30 ounces frog legs

Breading

2 cups vegetable oil for frying

2 cups corn flour

½ cup cornstarch

3 tablespoons Creole seasoning

½ teaspoon kosher salt, plus more for sprinkling

½ teaspoon freshly cracked black pepper, plus more for sprinkling

½ teaspoon cayenne pepper

1 teaspoon finely grated fresh lemon peel

FRIED FROGS LEGS

For the marinade, in a large bowl whisk together the egg, milk, garlic powder, onion powder, hot sauce, salt, and pepper until well blended. Add the frog legs and marinate for 1 hour.

For the breading, pour the oil 2 inches deep into a large Dutch oven or deep skillet. Heat over high heat to 355 degrees.

In a shallow bowl combine the corn flour, cornstarch, Creole seasoning, salt, pepper, cayenne, and lemon peel. Remove the frog legs from the marinade and dredge them in the breading.

Add a few frog legs to the hot oil and fry 5 minutes. They will begin to bubble slightly. Transfer the frog legs to a paper towel-lined plate and season with additional salt and pepper. Allow the oil to return to 355 degrees before cooking the next batch.

Serves 6.

Maddie's Café on the Square

Searcy, Arkansas

Maddie's Café on the Square in Searcy is pretty hard to miss despite its small size. The bright red-and-white awning that shades the entryway of this establishment brings to mind fond memories of the circus. Inside, however, there are no elephants with fancy headdresses or dancing tigers—just a small, open dining room with a beautiful hand-painted mural of the local historic spots. You can visit the whole town of Searcy just by sitting in the dining room of Maddie's.

Frequented by locals and students of Harding University, Maddie's is known for down-home comfort food. The favorite meal for locals and students alike is breakfast. Whether it's after an all-nighter of studying for a big exam or just a pre-Sunday school meal, breakfast always sounds good. And from the line of patrons waiting to be seated, I could tell the food would be tasty.

When I wandered into Maddie's, I was surrounded by some of the most deliciously simple kitchen smells you could ask for: frying bacon and pancakes on the griddle. After all my travels, there is something about a hot breakfast that makes me feel at home. Maybe it's because it's a meal I can almost guarantee that all four of my kids will eat without a fight. Or maybe it's because no matter where I am, eggs, bacon, and pancakes are so familiar.

Whatever the reason, I followed the masses and had breakfast for lunch. I picked scrambled eggs, a side of crispy bacon, some hash browns, and a short stack of pancakes. When my plate arrived, I was glad I stuck with the classics. With my cup of coffee in hand, I embarked on a delicious journey. As I ate, I was struck by the light and airy quality of the pancakes. They were slightly sweet, even without the syrup, and so tasty that I cleaned my plate before I even realized it. There's something to be said for taking something as simple as a pancake and elevating it to a level that was this memorable.

I've recreated my lighter-than-air pancake experience in the following recipe. Take time to enjoy these whenever you get the urge, because there's nothing like a little breakfast for dinner every now and then. And next time you're in Searcy, be sure to drop by Maddie's Café on the Square. I can promise you the food is worth the wait in line.

3 large eggs

3 tablespoons extra-fine sugar

2 cups all-purpose flour

1 ¼ teaspoons salt

2 teaspoons baking powder

2 cups milk

¼ cup butter, melted

Vegetable oil for cooking

PANCAKES

In a large bowl whisk the eggs and sugar together until creamed. Add the flour, salt, baking powder, milk, and butter, and whisk until blended.

Pour 1 tablespoon of oil into a large cast-iron skillet over medium heat. When the oil is hot, ladle 2 ounces of the batter per pancake into the skillet. When the batter edges begin to bubble, flip the pancakes over and cook until the pancakes are golden brown, about 3 to 4 minutes. Transfer the cooked pancake to a plate and keep warm in a 200-degree oven. Repeat the process until all the batter has been used.

Serves 8.

Mather Lodge Restaurant

Morrilton, Arkansas

f you know me at all, you know that I am not much of an outdoorsman. Don't get me wrong; I love being outside. I'm just not the guy who throws the poles in the back of the car and hikes to the perfect spot to set up my own campsite. But that doesn't mean that I don't enjoy the beauty of nature. I just like it with my creature comforts nearby. That leads me to my next destination on this journey: Petit Jean State Park. The park has breathtaking views and numerous hiking trails leading to beautiful scenery and waterfalls.

Mather Lodge is a place where I can enjoy the beauty of nature without having to sacrifice my own comfort. Renovated in 2012, the lodge has expanded its kitchen and dining room to accommodate more than 100 guests and visitors. The building's Adirondack-style architecture lends itself to beautiful views of the surrounding countryside. It's easy to relax and enjoy the view here, while taking in some tasty food.

Looking over the menu, I decided on a Southern classic: the chicken fried steak. This dish consists of a piece of beef pounded into a thin cutlet, breaded and fried in chicken grease. What could be more Southern than that? It's traditionally served with white gravy and mashed potatoes, which is just how the Mather Lodge chooses to showcase this specialty.

Chicken fried steak is the kind of stick-to-your-ribs food that hikers and other outdoorsy types need to keep their energy up in the great outdoors. For me, it's just a tasty treat. But who knows? Maybe if I eat this, I will get an urge to hike down the canyon and build my own fire. Or maybe not. Either way, I know my tummy will be full, and I will be happy.

When my plate arrived, it looked delicious, and in this case, looks were not deceiving. The breading had the perfect mix of salt and pepper and just the right amount of crunch without being overcooked. The white gravy was the icing on top of this grease-infused so-called steak. I dived in with knife and fork flying, as though I'd just hiked a mountain. When every last bite had disappeared, I sat back and admired my handiwork.

Recreate this crunchy, meaty goodness in your own kitchen, and who knows? Maybe you will be camping out with the other rugged crew, or maybe you will just enjoy a nice dinner with the family that will leave them all full and satisfied. It's a win-win either way. And if you'd like a little scenery to add to the mix, make a trip to Mather Lodge and take in the view.

1/3 cup all-purpose flour

1 teaspoon salt

Freshly cracked black pepper

1/4 teaspoon onion powder

1/8 teaspoon garlic powder

2 cups milk

1 large egg

1 teaspoon vinegar-based hot sauce

1 1/2 cups panko bread crumbs

4 cube steaks, pounded thin

1/3 cup all-purpose vegetable oil

CHICKEN FRIED STEAK

In a shallow bowl combine the flour, salt, pepper, onion powder, and garlic powder. In another shallow bowl whisk together the milk, egg, and hot sauce. In a third shallow bowl add the bread crumbs. Dredge the steaks in the flour mixture. Then dip them into the milk mixture to coat well. Finally, dredge the meat in the bread crumbs. Place the steaks on a baking sheet and refrigerate for 15 minutes.

Pour the oil into a large cast-iron skillet and heat over medium-high heat. Once the oil begins to shimmer, add the breaded meat and cook 2 minutes per side for medium-rare. For well-done steaks, continue cooking up to 6 minutes per side. This dish is best served with white gravy (page 243), a healthy dose of black pepper, and mashed potatoes (page 100).

Serves 4.

MeMe's Café

At MeMe's Café in Caraway, the owners and staff not only have their own family values but they encourage you in yours. On the MeMe's Facebook page, almost every post includes the line "Hug your babies!" or "Hug and kiss your babies!" reminding you, as your grandma would, to love on your kiddos. The motto of the restaurant (formerly known as The Feed Lot) is "Feeding the Community," and these folks take that to heart.

MeMe's daily specials are handwritten on a dry-erase white board in various colors, of course, to attract consumers' eyes. The menu offers all kinds of Southern fare, from fried chicken to hamburger steak to chicken and dressing. The homemade pies are good enough to make your grandma cry. I had a hard time making up my mind about what to choose.

The staff helped some with the daily entrée already chosen for me, but the list of sides was daunting. Faced with a choice of fried okra, baby carrots, creamed potatoes, and green beans, I felt as though I needed a clone so that I could try everything. I finally decided on the hamburger steak with white beans, fried okra, and green beans.

You have to admire a place that doesn't even refer to a vegetable by its name, but instead by its appearance. I find this to be common in the South. Pinto beans become "brown beans" and kidney beans become "red beans," while "white beans" can be any variation of cannellini beans, great northern beans, or navy beans. Thus was the story of my white beans side—and the show stealer for the day.

Like stew or chili on a cold winter day, there is something so satisfying and filling about a bowl of white beans. It warms the soul. The hot sauce I added copiously to the bowl didn't hurt the warming process either. The beans were cooked perfectly, soft, but not mushy, and seasoned well with just the right amount of salt and pepper. I enjoyed all the food I had at MeMe's in Caraway, but the recipe I'm giving to you is for the soul-satisfying white beans. And as MeMe always says, once you get that warm feeling in your belly, don't forget to "hug and kiss those babies!"

COUNTRY WHITE BEANS WITH SMOKED HAM HOCK

Fill a Dutch oven with 6 inches of water. Add the beans and bring to a boil over medium-high heat. Add the ham hock, salt, pepper, herb stems, bay leaves, and onion. Reduce the heat to low, cover, and simmer for 3 hours. Add water as needed to keep the beans covered during cooking.

Once the beans are cooked, remove the herbs and ham hock. Remove the meat from the ham hock, and roughly chop it. Return the meat to the beans. Serve the beans with plenty of the potlikker and hot sauce.

Serves 12.

4 cups dried white beans, cleaned

1 smoked ham hock

1 tablespoon kosher salt

1 tablespoon freshly cracked black pepper

1 handful parsley stems, bound with twine

2 bay leaves

1 medium white onion, roughly chopped

Hot sauce for serving

Miller's Cafeteria

Magnolia, Arkansas

Scott and Deena Hardin aren't your typical restaurant owners. The couple, up until 2011, were schoolteachers. The most restaurant experience the pair had between them was Scott's brief stint waiting tables in Little Rock, Arkansas, what seems like a lifetime ago to the couple. But when they met Corky Fantini, an old military buddy of Scott's father, while dining at Miller's Cafeteria and he mentioned he was ready for a change of pace, the couple decided to plunge into restaurants fulltime. They began negotiations to take over the restaurant from Fantini, feeling that the establishment had too much of a legacy to let it go by the wayside. Established in 1972 and operating in its current location since 1977 with only two owners, Miller's Cafeteria in Magnolia is somewhat of a fixture in the town.

The couple decided to keep the menu pretty much the same with additions such as a daily soup offering, especially in the colder months, and more catering and take-home offerings for customers. The place is fairly small with a single buffet bar that offers true Southern staples such as fruit salads, veggie salads, deviled eggs, and entrées such as chicken and dressing with gravy. There's a great mix of vegetables to choose from, including delicious squash casserole and sweet potato casserole. The prices are a nice break from today's overpriced restaurants, with the choice of a meat and two veggies totaling a mere $3.99—a much better value, if you ask me, than other so-called value meals.

One of the best parts of the restaurant, though, is the sweet little lady known as "Miss Mary." She has worked at Miller's Cafeteria since 1973, filling every role that you can imagine. She is now the restaurant manager and is known and beloved by all. She calls all her customers "baby" in true Southern style, and you can't help but feel as though she is your long-lost grandmother.

After meeting Miss Mary, I couldn't wait to dig into the food. I knew that it would be amazing and prepared with true Southern hospitality and love. I perused the vegetable offerings including turnip greens, creamed potatoes, lima beans, purple hull peas, and corn and finally settled on the fresh stewed okra with tomatoes. Okra is one of those dishes people tend to feel very strongly about. They either love it or hate it, and the feeling is almost always tied to the texture, not the taste. It takes skill to prepare okra in a way that doesn't leave the person eating it with a slimy surprise. At Miller's Cafeteria, the cooks have their technique down. The okra is delicious and tender, but not slimy, and the tomatoes give the dish just the right amount of acidity to kick up the flavor. When you make the recipe I've included here, be sure to follow the preparatory steps with the okra. Who knows? Maybe you might change someone's mind about it.

6 slices bacon, chopped

1 ½ cups minced yellow onion

1 tablespoon minced garlic

1 pound fresh okra, sliced

5 cups fresh tomatoes, chopped, with juice and seeds (3 to 4 large tomatoes)

1 teaspoon brown sugar

1 teaspoon kosher salt

½ teaspoon freshly cracked black pepper

Hot sauce to taste

TOMATOES AND STEWED OKRA

Heat a large skillet over high heat. Add the bacon and cook until crispy. Remove the bacon and place on a paper towel–lined plate to drain. Leave the grease in the pan.

Reduce the heat to medium and add the onions and garlic. Sauté until the onions become translucent, about 10 minutes. Add the okra and cook until the liquid from the okra begins to release, about 5 minutes.

Add the tomatoes with all the juices, sugar, salt, and pepper. Increase the heat to medium-high and bring to a boil. Cover, reduce the heat to low, and simmer for 20 minutes. Taste and adjust seasonings as needed and stir in the reserved bacon. Serve immediately.

Serves 10 to 12.

Natalie's Café and Catering

Batesville, Arkansas

When you walk up to Natalie's Café and Catering in Batesville, you may get a little confused. With the fleur de lis symbols and Mardi Gras masks decorating the outside sign, you may think you've wandered slightly off course and landed on Bourbon Street. There's a lot that's Creole about this place, and plenty Southern. The handwritten menu in bright colors welcomes you as soon as you walk in, and the offerings change frequently to keep customers guessing and coming back to see what's new.

The dining room is quaint and brightly colored in teals and purples, in keeping with the Louisiana style. There is a deli case showcasing Natalie's delicious prepared salads and ready-to-go casseroles. Business is busy, and the place hosts quite a few regulars. Strangely enough, nothing on the menu is fried, but that doesn't deter the local Southern customers; the food is tasty enough sans grease.

The owner, Natalie Cox, is a super sweet lady who wants to make sure her customers are happy and never leave hungry. She is frequently found in the dining room, smiling and greeting guests. She likes to be hands-on with her restaurant and makes her guests feel welcome and at home. She's the epitome of a Southern hostess and doles out hospitality freely.

As I looked over the menu, I was intrigued by the less well-known Southern dishes on the menu, such as Frito pie, mixed in with Louisiana favorites such as the shrimp po' boy. With so many different options, I have to say that Natalie has made it hard for her guests to pick a favorite dish. Maybe that is why her menu offers guests the "Salad Plate," a choice of three different side items.

Since I like to sample, I knew I had found the right choice for me. I picked the broccoli slaw, the Cajun chicken salad, and the crack corn dip. No, that's not a typo. It's not "cracked" corn dip; it's "crack" corn dip. When my plate arrived at the table, everything on it was tasty, but it wasn't until that moment that the true meaning of the name "crack corn dip" became apparent—this stuff was addictive.

I ate every last bite and felt like doing my best Oliver Twist impression and asking for more. Instead, I put that effort into recreating the recipe so I can enjoy the addictive creamy goodness of the crack corn dip anytime I want. So if you're passing through Batesville, don't hesitate to stop by Natalie's Café for some delicious Southern food, but before you order the corn dip, don't say I didn't warn you.

CRACK CORN DIP

2 (15-ounce) cans sweet corn, drained

1 (6-ounce) can green chilies, drained

1 (6-ounce) can tomatoes with green chilies, drained

1 ½ cups mayonnaise

1 ½ cups sour cream

1 ½ cups grated sharp Cheddar cheese

¾ cup shredded pepper jack cheese

1 cup minced green onions

1 cup seeded and minced jalapeño pepper

1 teaspoon garlic powder

1 teaspoon hot sauce

In a large bowl combine the corn, green chilies, tomatoes with green chilies, mayonnaise, sour cream, Cheddar cheese, pepper jack cheese, green onions, jalapeño, garlic powder, and hot sauce. Mix well with a rubber spatula until all the ingredients are well incorporated. Taste and adjust seasonings. Cover and refrigerate for 10 to 12 hours. Serve at room temperature or heat in the microwave or slowly bring to temperature and hold in a crockpot.

Serves 8.

NOTE: For 1 cup of dip, heat in the microwave for 45 to 60 seconds. Do not refrigerate after heating.

Opal Mae's Café

Russellville, Arkansas

When I think of a typical downtown area, I can't help but hear sirens in the background and picture some shady characters. But in small-town America, that's an unheard of scenario. Downtown is the heart of the town, well lit and inviting to those who live there and those just passing through. In Russellville, Opal Mae's Café epitomizes the meaning of the original downtown restaurant with open doors and welcoming smiles. The place is small, so you'd better come on an off-hour or early on the weekends, but it's a place that's worth the planning.

While I'm not fond of buffets in general, I was taken by surprise by the small buffet nestled in the cramped space of Opal Mae's Café. The lunch buffet is served with a choice of three entrées, twelve vegetables, salad, cornbread, and assorted desserts. There is also a separate lunch menu with entrées that are served with a choice of vegetable, salad, bread, and dessert. Since I had been traveling so much lately and I was, at this point, downright embarrassed to have to let out my belt another notch, I chose to skip the buffet option and order from the regular menu. I figured I would still get to taste the yummy goodness of the buffet, but would be self-limiting by ordering off of the menu.

That day the soup on the menu was corn chowder. For those of you not familiar with this delicious treat, corn chowder is a cream-based soup, similar to the Northern favorite, clam chowder. In this soup, corn is used instead of clams, and the base takes on the sweetness of the corn. It also usually includes potatoes and is frequently topped with bacon.

When the bowl arrived at my table, I smelled the creamy sweet goodness of the chowder and the savory hint of bacon. As "light" as soup is supposed to be, this one still had the creamy and savory notes I needed to come away feeling like I had a full meal. It gave me that home-cooked warmth in my tummy without making me feel as though I'll need a roll of antacids or another seat on the plane back home for my gut.

It's the simple things in life that I truly enjoy, and this soup definitely falls into that category. Corn chowder is not difficult to make, and when executed well it can impress even the toughest customer. So add this recipe to your repertoire, and if you happen to make a stop in Russellville, be sure to stop by Opal Mae's Café and thank the chef for your newfound culinary mastery.

CORN CHOWDER

In a large saucepan over medium heat, cook the bacon until brown and crispy. Remove the bacon and place it on a paper towel–lined plate to drain. Reserve the grease in the pan.

Add the onions, thyme leaves, salt, and pepper to the pan. Cook until the onions are translucent, about 8 to 10 minutes. Add the cream, potatoes, and 2 cups of the corn. Simmer until the potatoes are almost tender, about 20 minutes. Add the remaining 2 cups corn and cook for 10 minutes. Add ½ teaspoon nutmeg, stir, and taste for seasoning. Add additional salt, pepper, and nutmeg if desired. If not serving immediately, let cool completely at room temperature before refrigerating.

Serves 6 to 8.

6 slices bacon, diced

1 yellow onion, thinly sliced

2 teaspoons fresh thyme leaves

¾ teaspoon kosher salt

¼ teaspoon black pepper

4 cups heavy cream

2 large russet potatoes, peeled and cut into ½ inch cubes

4 cups fresh corn kernels, divided

½ teaspoon ground nutmeg, plus more to taste

Sue's Kitchen

Jonesboro, Arkansas

Traditional Southern towns have an interesting setup. Usually there is a courthouse in the middle of the downtown area, surrounded by storefronts on all four sides. For outsiders, navigating this square can be somewhat cumbersome, but for Southerners, it's just the norm. In Jonesboro, while wandering around the square, I stumbled across a hidden gem in what used to be the old post office: Sue's Kitchen.

Sue Robinson Williams is a little woman with a big passion for cooking and baking. She has retired, and her son, John Williams, now runs the joint, but you can still find her working in the restaurant on most days. She's one of those "I'm retired, but not retired" kind of folk who enjoys hard work too much to sit idly while others carry on her namesake restaurant. That kind of attitude commands respect in my book.

Sue's Kitchen is known for its delicious lunch and breakfast fare. And around the holidays, Sue's Kitchen can help ease your burden of additional mouths to feed with a holiday catering menu. When you walk into the restaurant, however, you are greeted by the true cherry on top—deli cases full of baked creations. The cakes are almost too pretty to eat, but I wouldn't want to offend, by any means.

For my lunch, I ordered the chef's daily special with three veggies, and I truly enjoyed every last bite. After loosening my belt, I perused the dessert menu. The caramel apple cake and the pink lemonade pie were very tempting, but I finally decided on the Italian crème coconut cake. With the richness and the butter and the toasted coconut, coconut cake is something that, to me, simply belongs in the South right next to a giant pitcher of sweet tea.

When the cake arrived, I was very pleased with my choice. The cake was rich and moist, and the crème frosting was perfect. That is everything you could possibly ask for in a cake. I put on my sweetest little boy act and tried to get Sue to give me the secret, but this little lady is a tough one and wouldn't share her recipe with an outsider. So, yet again, I am forced to toil away in the kitchen to recreate a delicious dessert. I hope you enjoy all my hard work, and if you happen to be in Jonesboro, stop by the old post office and pick up the best package ever—a tasty slice of one of Sue's desserts.

ITALIAN CRÈME COCONUT CAKE

For the cake, preheat the oven to 350 degrees. Grease and flour three 9-inch cake pans.

Place the shaved coconut in a shallow baking pan. Place the pecans in a second shallow pan. Bake the coconut and pecans for 5 minutes, or until the coconut is toasted and the pecans are lightly toasted and fragrant.

Place the butter and shortening in a large bowl, and beat with a hand mixer until fluffy. Gradually add the white sugar and brown sugar, beating well after each addition. Add the egg yolks one at a time, beating until blended after each addition. Add the vanilla.

In a medium bowl combine the flour and baking soda. Add the flour mixture and buttermilk alternately to the egg mixture, beating on low speed after each addition, just until blended.

Use a spatula to stir in half of the pecans and sweetened flaked coconut.

Place the egg whites in a large bowl and whip with a hand mixer on high speed until stiff peaks form. Fold into the batter. Divide the cake batter among the cake pans.

Bake the cakes for 25 minutes, or until a wooden pick inserted near the center comes out clean. Let the cakes cool in the pans on wire racks for 20 minutes before removing from the pans to cool completely on wire racks for about 45 minutes.

For the icing, in a large bowl beat the cream cheese and butter with a hand mixer on medium-high speed. Add the vanilla and powdered sugar, 1/2 cup at a time. Scrape the sides of the bowl and the beaters, and mix once more to ensure all the cream cheese lumps are incorporated.

To assemble the cake, place the first layer on a cake plate or stand and spread a portion of the icing on top. Place the second layer on top and cover with additional icing. Place the final layer on top and spread the remaining icing on the top and sides of the cake. Gently press the toasted shaved coconut and the remaining pecans onto the sides of the cake.

Serves 10 to 12.

Cake

3 cups shaved dried coconut

1 1/4 cups finely chopped pecans

3/4 cup butter, softened

1/2 cup vegetable shortening

2 cups white sugar

1/2 cup packed dark brown sugar

5 large eggs, at room temperature and separated

1 tablespoon vanilla extract

2 1/4 cups all-purpose flour

1 1/8 teaspoons baking soda

1 1/4 cups buttermilk

1 cup sweetened flaked coconut

Cream Cheese Icing

16 ounces cream cheese, softened

1 cup (2 sticks) butter, softened

1 teaspoon vanilla extract

2 pounds powdered sugar

GUEST CHECK
7 2
mac
coll
rutas
swpot 175
64625
GUEST CHECK
7 2 64624
Wht CKN 650
coll 170
yam
bep
side of wht
Wht CKN 650
limas
R/Wht
64624

GEORGIA

One of the things I have really enjoyed about writing this book is traveling to places so rich in history and tradition. Georgia is definitely a true Southern gem, steeped in heritage and history, the last of the original thirteen colonies and the fourth state in the U.S.A. Georgia is known as the Peach State, and the connection to the fruit has led many in the Southeast to refer to a lovely Georgian young lady as a true "Georgia peach."

The state of Georgia has a very diverse landscape with mountains in the northeastern part, piedmont and midlands in the middle, and the coast on the southeastern tip. The weather is the perfect mix of mild winters and hot, semi-humid summers. With beautiful landscapes everywhere you turn, the people in this state tend to prefer the outdoors most of the time, and if you visit, you will see why.

Despite its Peach State moniker, Georgia's main crop is peanuts. The state produces almost half of the nation's peanuts annually. The people here are hands-on with the outdoors and agriculture, and one out of every seven Georgians works in agriculture, forestry, or a related industry. It's no wonder that the state has such great meat and three restaurants with its residents being so closely tied to the land. Don't get me wrong, though. Georgia isn't all farmhands and forest rangers.

You can't talk about Georgia without bringing up its musical ties or, if you're like me, without hearing the state song "Georgia on My Mind" playing in your head. A close second is Gladys Knight and the Pips singing "Midnight Train to Georgia." But the music didn't stop there. It carried into the 1990s with bands such as R.E.M. and the B-52s and continues to this day with such soulful artists as John Mayer.

Georgia has been home to many famous and inspiring people, including Martin Luther King, Jr., Ray Charles, Juliette Gordon Low (the founder of the Girls Scouts), and Dr. John S. Pemberton (the inventor of Coca-Cola), among others. The state seems to produce people who are natural leaders in whatever field they enter, whether it's music, politics, sports, or scientific innovation. The people of Georgia are determined to make things better in one way or another. I encountered this mindset often in my travels throughout the great state, meeting the proprietors and operators of meat and three restaurants along the way. From the time-tested institutions such as Mary Mac's Tea Room in Atlanta to the pop culture referenced Weaver D's in Athens, Georgia had a story to tell, and I was eager to listen and, of course, to get my fill of delicious food along the way. The next time you're planning a trip and looking for a place that has a rich history, beautiful landscapes, interesting people, a generous helping of Southern hospitality, and delicious home cooking, add Georgia to the list. You will thank me.

Busy Bee Café

Atlanta, Georgia

I n 1947 Lucy Jackson opened the doors of the Busy Bee Café in downtown Atlanta. Lucy was a self-taught cook who wanted to bring people joy through delicious soul food. There's a story of Lucy feeding an African missionary who was unable to afford a meal at another establishment. Per the legend, the missionary bestowed blessings upon Lucy's business, stating that it would always be busy, thus cementing the name "Busy Bee."

After running her own restaurant for more than twenty years, Lucy retired and sold the business to a couple of investors. One of the investors handed over the reigns of the restaurant to his daughter, Tracy Gates, who has been running the business since 1985. Tracy carries on in Lucy's time-honored tradition of cooking Southern food with passion and love. She has even coined the word "bee-licious" to describe the food at this joint to convey that the deliciousness you enjoy here is unique to this location.

On the walls the pictures of famous people who have stopped by the Busy Bee to enjoy a meal tell me that I'm in the right place for some fantastic food. The service staff moves quickly, which is a good thing since this place is extremely busy. The hum of the crowd sounds a little like a beehive, come to think of it. I settle into a booth and look over the menu, which includes Southern favorites along with specials that change daily.

I had heard that the fried chicken at the Busy Bee is the stuff of legends, and I was tempted to go for it. But the smothered chicken caught my eye—two pieces of fried chicken smothered in pan gravy. I topped it off with a carrot soufflé and string beans with potatoes.

When my plate arrived, I understood how the owner is confident enough to proclaim her food "bee-licious." The smells coming from my plate made my mouth water. As I dug into the chicken, my stomach sang a hymn of praise. The chicken was well marinated before hitting the fryer. Then the cook smothered it with a perfectly seasoned pan gravy and simmered it until it nearly melted in my mouth.

I begged Tracy for her trade secrets, but that queen bee wasn't about to spill the beans. I've recreated the dish in the following recipe, and I don't think you'll be disappointed. If you happen to be in Atlanta, though, stop by the Busy Bee and try it for yourself. Your taste buds will thank me.

SMOTHERED CHICKEN

Sprinkle the chicken on both sides with 1 teaspoon of salt and ½ teaspoon of black pepper.

Place the vegetable oil in a large skillet and heat over medium-high heat. When the oil is smoking hot, add the chicken breasts and sear for 5 minutes undisturbed. Turn the breasts over and sear for 3 minutes. Transfer the chicken to a baking pan.

Wipe the skillet clean with a paper towel, add the bacon to the pan and render until crispy. Remove the bacon to a paper towel–lined plate to drain, leaving the drippings in the pan. Add the mushrooms, onions, garlic, celery, and carrots to the bacon grease and cook over medium heat until the vegetables are softened, 5 to 7 minutes. Add the butter and flour to the vegetable mixture and cook, stirring, for 1 minute. Pour in the heavy cream and milk while whisking. Increase the heat to medium-high and bring the sauce to a full boil. Reduce the heat to medium-low and slowly add the chicken stock while constantly whisking. Add the remaining 1 teaspoon of salt and ½ teaspoon of black pepper and carefully slide the chicken breasts back into the pan. Cover the pan and reduce the heat to low. Cook for 20 minutes, stirring occasionally.

Crumble the bacon and add it to the pan. Spoon an ample amount of gravy and vegetables over each breast. Freeze any remaining sauce to use as the base for a quick smothered chicken dinner.

Serves 2.

2 (6- to 8-ounce) boneless, skinless chicken breasts

2 teaspoons salt, divided

1 teaspoon black pepper, ground, divided

4 tablespoons vegetable oil

4 slices thick-cut bacon, diced

1 cup sliced white mushrooms

½ cup minced yellow onion

2 cloves garlic, minced

¼ cup finely chopped celery

¼ cup finely chopped carrots

2 tablespoons butter

½ cup all-purpose flour

½ cup heavy cream

½ cup whole milk

2 cups chicken stock

Freshly cracked black pepper to taste

Doug's Place

Emerson, Georgia

Doug's Place in Emerson is somewhat of a strange architectural arrangement. The building looks as if someone took an old red barn and attached a screened-in porch to the front. It's not the sturdiest looking construction I've seen on my travels, but sometimes you've got to live on the edge, so I headed inside. The interior is simple with tables scattered throughout and red vinyl booths. It's the perfect "hole-in-the-wall" kind of find that you can surprise your friends with once they taste the food.

Locals guided me to this joint. After navigating the plethora of potholes in the gravel parking lot, I cautiously walked in and chose my seat. The mood was mellow, but the staff seemed to be moving quickly to serve everyone's needs. The walls were peppered with old black-and-white pictures, letting me know that this place had been around awhile. The waitress was pleasant and handed me a daily menu to make my choice for lunch. The locals swore by the veggie plate here, so I looked over the sides. It was a vegetable wonderland with more than a dozen choices.

I decided on chicken and dumplings, seasoned green beans, and pineapple cream cheese salad with a side of the homemade cornbread. When my plate arrived, the steam coming off of the chicken and dumplings made me feel warm inside. The cornbread was moist and sweet, the perfect complement to the beans and the dumplings.

After wolfing down the hot food, I welcomed the cool, sweet treat of the pineapple cream cheese salad. Fruit salads are widespread in the South, and if you don't have some sweetness to them, you might as well just skip them altogether. The salad really finished off the meal nicely. I've included the simple recipe for this sweet treat below so you can be a hit at the next potluck or backyard barbecue. And if you happen to pass through Emerson, remember, don't judge a book by its cover, and stop by Doug's Place for some tasty grub.

PINEAPPLE CREAM CHEESE SALAD

Drain the pineapple and oranges, reserving the juices to thin the salad as needed.

Place the pineapple, oranges, apples, pears, and marshmallows in a large bowl and toss well.

In a medium bowl beat the cream cheese and powdered sugar with a hand mixer on medium speed. Add the coconut, pecans, and salt. Fold the cream cheese mixture into the fruit and marshmallow mixture until well incorporated. Pour into individual serving cups or a medium nonstick casserole dish. Refrigerate overnight and serve with additional toasted coconut flakes and pecans as a garnish.

Serves 10 to 12.

1 (20-ounce) can diced pineapple

1 cup mandarin oranges

1 apple, peeled and finely chopped

1 pear, peeled and finely chopped

1 cup miniature marshmallows

1 (8-ounce) package cream cheese, softened

½ cup powdered sugar

2 tablespoons sweetened flaked coconut, toasted, plus more for garnish

2 tablespoons chopped pecans, toasted, plus more for garnish

1 teaspoon kosher salt

Eats Restaurant

Atlanta, Georgia

It's not often you will find a meat and three restaurant in the South known for its jerk chicken, but Eats Restaurant in Atlanta is known for just that. Opened in 1993 by Robert Hatcher and Charles Kerns, the restaurant has become an Atlanta mainstay with eclectic options that play on the meat and three angle. The "meat" staple here is the chicken, but you can also find a turkey meatloaf or, on Fridays, jerk tilapia.

The place is known for serving up delicious grub at a very reasonable price, and if you're like me, you can totally appreciate that. Prices start at just under six bucks for a veggie-only plate and hit the ceiling at all of eight bucks for a traditional meat and three plate.

Although I don't usually like to follow the crowd when it comes to dining, I had to try the jerk chicken. I went for the high-dollar meal and chose corn on the cob, black-eyed peas, and broccoli casserole as my three sides.

The tender, juicy chicken was amazing—spicy, but amazing—and, boy, was I glad to have a giant glass of iced tea handy to help me along my way. The veggies were delicious, and the starches were the perfect complement to quiet the fire in my mouth. I nearly licked my plate clean and was very glad that I had gone for the "big boy" platter.

As I was leaving, I couldn't help noticing the homemade brownies packaged in plastic wrap next to the cash register. They were calling my name, begging me to indulge in their chocolate goodness. Although my willpower is very strong, the siren's song of the brownies was just too much for me that day, and I gave in.

The brownie was delicious, and I was glad to have been seduced by its chocolaty call. It was moist and sweet, the perfect finish for my spicy chicken treat. I certainly wanted to share those brownies with my kids, so I spent some time in the kitchen recreating the recipe and hope that you enjoy my efforts. If you get a chance to pop into Eats Restaurant in Atlanta, don't hesitate to try the jerk chicken, but be sure to save room for an amazing homemade brownie.

HOMEMADE CHOCOLATE BROWNIES

Preheat the oven to 375 degrees. Grease a 9 x 13-inch baking pan.

In a medium saucepan over low heat, combine the butter and sugar. Cook for 2 minutes, stirring constantly. Do not let the mixture boil. Pour the butter mixture into a large bowl. Gradually add the cocoa powder, and beat with a hand mixer on medium speed to blend. Add the eggs, salt, baking powder, espresso powder, and vanilla extract. Beat until well blended. Gradually stir in the flour until evenly mixed. Fold in the chocolate chunks and allow the batter to stand at room temperature for 30 minutes before baking.

Spread the batter evenly in the baking pan and bake for 30 minutes. The edges should be slightly crispy, and the center should still look moist. Let cool in the pan for 1 hour before cutting into squares and serving.

Serves 12.

1 ½ cups butter, softened

2 ½ cups sugar

1 ¼ cups cocoa powder

4 large eggs, beaten

2 teaspoons salt

1 ¼ teaspoons baking powder

2 ¼ teaspoons espresso powder

1 ½ tablespoons vanilla extract

2 cups all-purpose flour

2 cups semisweet chocolate chunks

Food for the Soul

Athens, Georgia

Call me a cheapskate, but I love finding great places where you can eat good food and fill up for less than ten bucks. When I asked the locals I met in Athens for a good recommendation for a home-cooked meal that wouldn't break the bank, they unanimously pointed me in the direction of Food for the Soul. This is a no-frills kind of place. The "good china" here is the divided Styrofoam plate complete with plastic cutlery.

Offering down-home Southern favorites that change daily, the buffet is large enough to hold four or five entrée options, six or seven sides, cornbread muffins, and dinner rolls. There is limited seating, so you may have to sit next to a stranger, but according to the locals, it's worth giving up the personal space to enjoy the food.

The current owner, Harold Henderson, runs the place with his mother, sister, brother, and nephew. They are a really nice group of folks, willing to leave you alone, but really friendly if you seek them out. There's not much ambiance to the place, but the food here is enough to keep the guests' attention it seems.

I decided to go for the all-you-can-eat option so that I could sample a little bit of everything that day. The place wasn't too crowded, so I grabbed a plate and started my tour-de-buffet. The fried chicken and fried pork chops were delicious. The owners definitely had the spice mix down.

My favorite part was the veggies. The sides—ranging from boiled cabbage to black-eyed peas to collard greens—were all fresh and tasted amazing, but the one that captured my attention was the stewed tomatoes. I could tell that they used tomatoes at the peak of ripeness. They were soft, but still intact with the perfect mix of sweet and tart that comes from taking the time to slow-cook them.

I recreated the effect in my recipe so that you can get a taste of the goodness I enjoyed that day. Be sure to take advantage of tomato season and catch them when they're at their peak. And if you get a chance to travel through Athens, don't pass up the Food for the Soul restaurant—you'll thank me later.

STEWED TOMATOES

Bring a large pot of water to a boil over high heat. Cut a small x on the bottoms of the tomatoes, just through the skin, but not into the flesh. Prepare a large bowl with water and ice and set aside.

Submerge the tomatoes in the simmering water for 60 seconds. Remove quickly and place in the ice bath. Let sit for 30 seconds, or until the skin is wrinkly and easily peels. Discard the skins and roughly chop the tomatoes.

In a large heavy-bottomed pot over medium heat, combine the tomatoes and their juices, salt, sugar, basil, bell pepper, and onion. Cook for 30 to 45 minutes. Serve immediately or freeze.

Serves 12.

12 large beefsteak tomatoes

2 teaspoons salt

2 teaspoons sugar

3 teaspoons dried basil

½ cup chopped green bell pepper

½ cup chopped Vidalia onion

Gladys Knight's Chicken & Waffles

Atlanta, Georgia

Restaurants with connections to stars don't usually impress me, unless the stars are well-known chefs. But Gladys Knight's Chicken & Waffles in Atlanta may get me to change my tune. Established in 1997, the restaurant is the brainchild of the singer's son, Shanga Hankerson. Shanga gained a love for the food industry while working in a butcher shop in Detroit, Michigan. The family had a brief run at the restaurant business, which didn't end well in the early days. With lessons learned and experience to share, Shanga pushed forward with his dream to have a restaurant while honoring his mother's legacy.

Chicken and waffles may seem like a strange mix if you've never tried it, and you may imagine that the dish originated in the South because of the link to fried chicken. However, chicken and waffles is said to have originated in Harlem in the 1930s at a small supper club frequented by celebrities who came in for late-night grub after closing down the jazz establishments. The customers couldn't decide on breakfast or dinner, so the owner of the club, Dickie Wells, came up with chicken and waffles to meet both desires.

I could feel the vibe of those jazz-filled nights in the ambiance at Gladys Knight's Chicken & Waffles. With dim lighting, lush leather booths, and dark wood walls peppered with pictures of Gladys and some of her gold records, the restaurant isn't your typical Southern greasy spoon. I slid into one of the booths and perused the menu.

The place offers a fusion of Southern soul food and contemporary dishes, with such novel appetizers as collard green spring rolls and catfish sliders. The buzz in this place is about the waffles, though, so I stayed the course and ordered the "Midnight Train," four fried chicken wings with one original waffle. I pictured myself walking out of a jazz club just past two o'clock in the morning and being in the mood for just such a treat.

When my plate arrived, I was happy that I did not stray. The wings were crisp and seasoned well, but it was the waffle that stole the show. The batter was the perfect combination of light, airy, and sweet, and the waffle had a great texture with just the right amount of crunch. I've tried to replicate the recipe and know that it will go over well with the harshest of critics—my children. Don't hesitate to stop by Gladys Knight's Chicken & Waffles the next time you pass through Atlanta and help yourself to a late-night or mid-morning plate of goodness.

BUTTERMILK WAFFLES

Place the eggs in a large bowl and whisk until blended. Add the buttermilk, butter, and vanilla, whisking until well mixed. In a medium bowl whisk together the flour, almond flour, sugar, baking powder, baking soda, and salt. Add the flour mixture to the egg mixture and whisk until perfectly smooth. (Do not over whisk.)

Spray an 8-inch waffle iron with cooking spray and spoon about ½ cup of the batter onto the grates. Cook for 3 to 4 minutes, until the waffle is golden brown and releases from both sides of the iron. Repeat with the remaining batter.

Serves 8.

3 large eggs

2 cups cold buttermilk

¾ cup butter, melted and cooled

2 teaspoons vanilla extract

2 ¼ cups all-purpose flour

1 cup almond flour

2 ½ tablespoons sugar

2 ¼ teaspoons baking powder

1 ¼ teaspoons baking soda

2 teaspoons salt

Cooking spray

Mary Mac's Tea Room

Atlanta, Georgia

Very few restaurants are able to last five years, much less sixty-five years, but in Atlanta, Mary Mac's Tea Room has done just that. Opened in 1945 by Mary McKenzie, the restaurant was called a "tea room," since women were frowned upon for owning their own businesses in those days, including restaurants. Mary opened the place to try to make money in the tough economic times following World War II, and it seemed to work well.

In the early 1960s, Margaret Lupo purchased the tea room and spent the next thirty years expanding the business from one small dining room to the grand restaurant it is today, complete with six dining rooms and a full-service bar. In 1994 Margaret hand-picked her successor, John Ferrell, to continue the tradition of Southern hospitality and good food.

It's not hard to see that this place is steeped in traditions, some typical Southern standards and some very unique. Take, for example, the place's "goodwill ambassador," Jo Carter. This nice lady makes her way around the dining room, giving out free back rubs. I'm not much of a touchy-feely person myself, especially with strangers, but even I can appreciate the sentiment here.

As I looked over the menu, I knew that I wouldn't be disappointed with whatever I ordered and that these recipes had been time-tested by millions before me. I decided on the roast pork with cornbread dressing, pork gravy, and cranberry sauce. Just writing the words now makes my mouth water. I mentioned to the waitress that this was my first time here at Mary Mac's, and she nearly squealed with delight. She delivered my basket of warm fresh bread, and to my surprise the basket was brimming with cinnamon rolls, corn bread, and yeast rolls. Cinnamon rolls? This must be a ploy to satisfy first-time customers.

From the moment I walked into the legendary Mary Mac's, I knew I was in for a wonderful Southern meal. They had me at sweet tea and hooked me on the roasted pork and cornbread dressing, but the sweet, fresh cinnamon rolls stole the show. When you're in Atlanta, be sure to drop by Mary Mac's Tea Room for some Southern hospitality and maybe even a back rub, because it doesn't get much better than this.

Cinnamon Rolls (page 66)

2 cups warm half and half (110 degrees F)

1 cup plus 1 tablespoon white sugar, divided

1 tablespoon plus 2 ¼ teaspoons yeast

9 ⅓ cups bread flour

2 teaspoons salt

4 whole eggs plus 1 yolk, at room temperature, whisked

⅔ cup plus 1 teaspoon butter, melted

Filling

⅔ cup butter, softened

2 cups plus 1 tablespoon packed brown sugar

⅓ cup ground cinnamon

Icing

2 (3-ounce) packages cream cheese, softened

½ cup plus 1 teaspoon butter, softened

3 cups plus 2 tablespoons powdered sugar

1 teaspoon vanilla extract

¼ teaspoon salt

CINNAMON ROLLS

For the dough, in a medium bowl whisk the warm half and half, 1 tablespoon of sugar, and the yeast. Cover with plastic wrap and set aside for ten minutes, until the yeast is actively bubbly. In a mixer with a dough hook attachment add the flour, salt, and remaining 1 cup sugar and mix at a low speed. Add the whisked eggs to the half and half yeast mixture and slowly pour into the dry ingredients. Increase to medium speed and mix until the dough releases from the sides of the mixing bowl, 3 to 5 minutes. Turn the dough ball out onto a floured work surface and cover with plastic; allow the dough to proof (rise) and double in size for 20 to 30 minutes. (The dough will proof quicker in a warm area of the kitchen.) Roll the proofed dough into a large rectangle 16 x 21 x 1-inch thick.

For the filling, spread the softened butter evenly across the entire dough sheet. In a small bowl combine the brown sugar and cinnamon and spread over the butter.

From the long end of the dough sheet roll the dough up, crimping each roll as you turn the entire log. Cut off and remove the uneven ends. Portion the cinnamon rolls by cutting across the dough log in 2-inch sections. Place the rolls in a baking pan top-side spiral up. Cover loosely with plastic wrap and allow to proof for a second time, about 30 minutes.

While the dough is proofing preheat the oven to 400 degrees and position a rack in the center. Bake the rolls until golden brown, 15 to 20 minutes.

While the rolls are baking prepare the icing. In a large bowl use a hand mixer to beat together the softened cream cheese, butter, powdered sugar, vanilla extract, and salt. When the cinnamon rolls are completely cooled spread or pipe the frosting generously on the rolls.

Serves 24.

Paschal's Restaurant

Atlanta, Georgia

Atlanta is one of those Southern cities that is steeped in history and heritage but also moving quickly with the times, and Paschal's Restaurant has followed that trend. Entrepreneurs James and Robert Paschal opened the restaurant in 1947 and knit themselves into the very fabric of the community they served. Paschal's has not only survived but thrived through many tumultuous events, including the civil rights movement, standing firm in its commitment to its patrons.

The building itself doesn't quite meet the typical mold of Southern meat and three restaurants. It's a large brick building with high ceilings, exposed ductwork, and lots of natural light from the multiple-level windows. The decor is laid back, with upscale touches that seem to meld the old and the new.

The restaurant has hosted prominent historical figures, such as Dr. Martin Luther King, Jr., and Dizzie Gillespie, and notable politicians, such as Hillary Clinton. The menu has gone through some changes but still offers traditional Southern fare with a modern touch, including fried chicken, fried green tomatoes, collard greens, and candied yams.

As I looked over the menu, I allowed myself to soak in the atmosphere and the history of the place. I happened upon Paschal's at lunchtime when it was buzzing with energy and filled with hungry customers. The ones already eating looked pleased, so I took that as a good sign. I decided to go for something from the Southern cuisine portion of the menu. Everything looked delicious, but I finally settled on the half herb roasted chicken with a side of cornbread dressing. Cornbread dressing is popular in the Southeast, in part because it makes use of leftover cornbread. It has become a staple at Southern holiday dinners and is a perennial favorite of the meat and three crowd.

When my lunch arrived, I was slightly overwhelmed by the amount of chicken on my plate. When they say half a chicken at this joint, they mean it. The meat was tender and juicy, and the herbs were a perfect complement. The cornbread dressing, though, is what I remember the most. It was just the right mix of butter, herbs, and moisture to really make the meal complete. I've done my best to recreate the recipe for you to share with your loved ones at the holidays or any time of year. If you happen to be in the Atlanta area, drop by Paschal's for the cornbread dressing and soak in the history.

1 tablespoon butter, softened

2 tablespoons vegetable oil

1 medium yellow onion, minced

2 carrots, peeled and finely chopped

2 celery ribs, minced

4 garlic cloves, minced

2 large eggs, whisked

1 (1-pound) loaf cornbread, cubed

3 cups chicken stock

1 teaspoon fresh rosemary, minced

1 teaspoon dried sage

2 hard-boiled eggs, grated

2 teaspoons salt, plus more for sprinkling on top

Freshly cracked black pepper to taste

1 tablespoon butter, melted

CORNBREAD DRESSING

Preheat the oven to 350 degrees. Grease a large cast-iron skillet with butter and place in the oven while you prepare the cornbread dressing.

Pour the oil into another large skillet and heat over medium-high. Add the onions and cook until golden brown, 5 to 7 minutes. Add the carrots and celery and cook for an additional 8 minutes. Stir in the garlic and cook 1 minute. Remove the pan from the heat.

In a large bowl add the whisked eggs, cubed cornbread, stock, rosemary, and sage. Mix together and add the warm vegetables and grated eggs. Stir to combine. Add the salt and pepper.

Remove the hot skillet from the oven and pour in the cornbread mixture. Cover with aluminum foil and bake for 20 minutes. Remove the foil, increase the temperature to 400 degrees, and cook for an additional 7 to 10 minutes, until the top is golden brown. Brush the top with melted butter and sprinkle with additional salt to taste.

Serves 10 to 12.

The Colonnade Restaurant

Atlanta, Georgia

In the restaurant business, there are two ways to roll with the ups and downs of the hospitality industry—serve truly great food that your loyal customers love or be flexible enough to add new tricks to your repertoire as tastes and trends change. At the Colonnade Restaurant in Atlanta, the owners have somehow managed to do both. Opened in 1927, the restaurant was housed in a small white-columned house until it lost its lease in 1962. Frank Tarleton, the owner at the time, had built a loyal customer base, and despite moving to a new location, the customers kept coming.

In 1979, the Colonnade was sold to the Jones family who expanded the restaurant to serve nearly 200 patrons. They still own the joint today and keep up with the ever-changing food trends by hiring innovative chefs who bring novel items to the menu while still maintaining the integrity of the time-tested recipes. You are likely to find kangaroo as a dinner special alongside familiar favorites such as fried pork chops.

Although it may seem as though the two food styles can't peacefully coexist under one roof, somehow the Colonnade pulls it off. This place isn't suffering from a split personality; it is able to serve both old and new customers without trying to be something it's not. That takes talent, and I couldn't wait to dig in to see what all the fuss is about.

As I looked over the menu, it took me a little longer than usual to decide. I didn't think I would be unhappy with choosing anything but finally settled on the braised short ribs of beef with Brussels sprouts and the sweet potato soufflé. When my plate arrived, I knew I wouldn't be let down. The meat was perfectly seasoned and very tender, nearly melting in my mouth. The sweet potato soufflé was a perfect contrast to the savory short ribs, but it was the Brussels sprouts that made me want to pat the chef on the back.

Brussels sprouts get a bad rap when they're poorly prepared. I am a huge fan of this veggie and know that, when prepared properly, they can be a delicious treat. At the Colonnade they were tender without being too soft and had the perfect mix of salt and pepper. I've included my recipe for you to enjoy at home. Who knows? Maybe you can convert your kids into Brussels sprout fans. Swing by the Colonnade Restaurant in Atlanta and give them a try.

BRUSSELS SPROUTS

Wash the Brussels sprouts, and trim off the bottoms with a small paring knife. Shake dry and cut each sprout in half lengthwise.

Heat a large sauté pan or cast-iron skillet over medium-high heat. Add the bacon and cook until crispy, 10 to 12 minutes. Transfer the bacon to a paper towel–lined plate to drain. Reserve the drippings in the pan. Add the Brussels sprouts to the pan, and increase the heat to high. Carefully add the water. Watch out for the steam. Cover and cook until the pan is dry, 4 to 6 minutes. Uncover and add the onion, garlic, lemon peel, red pepper flakes, molasses, and vinegar. Cook until all the flavors are well incorporated and aromatic. Season with salt and pepper, and serve immediately.

Serves 6.

1 pound fresh Brussels sprouts, about 30 pieces

½ pound bacon, cooked and chopped

¼ cup water

½ Vidalia onion, minced

1 clove garlic, crushed

1 teaspoon finely grated lemon peel

½ teaspoon crushed red pepper flakes

2 tablespoons sorghum molasses

1 tablespoon rice wine vinegar

Kosher salt and freshly cracked black pepper to taste

Weaver D's

Athens, Georgia

love a restaurant that has become such a fixture that it has invaded even the pop culture. The folks at Weaver D's in Athens have done just that. The building itself can't be missed, with its lime green paint job. It may be slightly off the beaten path for some travelers, but it's well worth the detour.

The place gained some notoriety in the 1990s when the Georgia-based band R.E.M. made the restaurant's slogan, "Automatic for the People," famous. The owner has acknowledged the band by adorning the walls inside with some R.E.M. memorabilia, but the joint maintains a very hometown feel. There's no coattail riding going on here.

The building is small with communal seating inside at four or five square-top tables and a few two-tops. The simple menu is on the wall with the push-pin type letters that someone painstakingly uses to spell out the choices. There are no frivolities here, with vinyl tablecloths covering each table, topped off with several condiment choices for the customer's pleasure, including chow-chow and, of course, hot sauce.

The owner and chef, Dexter Weaver, learned to cook from his mother and stepfather.

He is known in his community for being quite a character with a personality much larger than his tiny establishment. The menu itself is small, but packed full of Southern favorites such as fried chicken, pork chops, and chicken and dumplings.

The day I was there, the place was busy but moving steadily. The smells coming from the kitchen were delicious, and I couldn't wait to taste the food. I took my time and decided on the pork chops with collard greens, okra fritters, and the skillet cornbread. My food arrived piping hot in a short amount of time, and the aromas only got better up close and personal.

I devoured my food. The pork chops were tender and seasoned well, and the cornbread had just the right amount of sweetness to balance the vinegar flavor of the collard greens. The real treat and surprise, though, were the okra fritters. They were fried to a golden brown and had the perfect texture of soft and crunchy all rolled into one. Back home in my own kitchen, I recreated the magic they bestowed upon me that day and hope that I have done them justice. If you get a chance to drop by Weaver D's in Athens, don't hesitate to try out the original.

OKRA FRITTERS

Heat 1 tablespoon of vegetable oil in a deep frying skillet or cast-iron pan over medium heat. Add the onions and cook until translucent, 7 to 9 minutes. Remove the pan from the heat and set aside to cool at room temperature.

In a large bowl place the cornmeal, flour, baking powder, salt, and pepper and stir together. In a small bowl whisk the eggs and add the honey and water. Slowly whisk the egg mixture into the flour mixture until a batter forms. Stir in the cooled onions.

Pour 2 inches of oil into a large skillet over medium-high heat.

Place the okra in the bowl of a food processor and pulse until it's roughly chopped and creamy. The seeds and texture of the okra will create a natural binder.

When the oil is hot, portion 2 tablespoons of the batter per fritter into the oil. Repeat this process until the pan is full but not crowded. Spoon 1 tablespoon of the chopped okra on top of each fritter and season each with a pinch of salt. Once the batter bubbles and browns around the edges, flip the fritters over and cook until golden brown, about 2 minutes. Remove the fritters to a paper towel–lined plate. Add additional salt and pepper while the fritters are warm and serve immediately.

Serves 10 to 12.

2 cups vegetable oil, plus more for frying

1 cup diced sweet onion

1 cup cornmeal

½ cup all-purpose flour

1 teaspoon baking powder

2 teaspoons kosher salt, plus more for sprinkling

¼ teaspoon black pepper

2 large eggs

2 tablespoons honey

1 teaspoon water

3 cups sliced okra, fresh or frozen and thawed

Whistle Stop Café

Juliette, Georgia

The story of the Whistle Stop Café begins in Juliette in 1927, when Edward L. Williams opened his general store. After operating the store for more than forty-five years, Williams closed it in 1972 without notice and with only a few words to sum it all up: "I have had enough." But that wasn't the end for the old building. In 1991, it served as the location of the beloved Whistle Stop Café in the movie *Fried Green Tomatoes*, based on the book of the same name by Fannie Flagg. Once the filming was over, there was one more life in store for the building: Robert Williams, who had inherited it, opened a very real, nonfiction restaurant called the Original Whistle Stop Café.

Although the location has changed and there are multiple Whistle Stop cafes all over the state of Georgia, the one in Juliette is a favorite of locals and visitors alike with a menu that reflects a more simple time in Southern food. With a meat and three-style breakfast, lunch, and supper menu, there are few items I wouldn't recommend. As easy as it would be to gravitate toward the fried green tomatoes here, I fell in love with many other items, such as the fried okra, stewed squash, and field peas—all tasty, seasonal, and local. All the veggies were cooked with care, exactly the way I'd imagine my grandmother would have done.

I found this café by accident, and I'm thankful I did. I'm reminded that the book and movie *Fried Green Tomatoes* in many ways represent the theme of my book—the traditions and meaningful family bonds created through sharing a meal.

The locals spill into the building when the doors open each morning to snag a seat before the lines begin. Being a visitor, I unfortunately wasn't aware of the how quickly the line can form, but with patience and an empty stomach I waited for my chance. When it was my turn, I devoured each bite. It was pure self-control that kept me from ordering the entire selection on starters and sides. I settled into my first plate, and it was a home run. The Crispy Matchstick Sweet Potato Fries is a dish I hadn't seen in any other restaurant on this eating road trip bender. Imagine sweet potato fries, but maybe more like a matchstick, liberally dusted with cinnamon, sugar, and salt. It's a heavenly experience when someone fries the perfect potato—never soggy, always crispy, but not dry. The added sweet, salty, and savory flavors made it impossible for me to stop before the entire plate was empty.

While I don't know the trick to their magical abilities of frying sweet potatoes cut so thin, here is the recipe I've created that best captures the sweet potato experience. If you find yourself hungry for Southern food and a true Southern experience, make it a point to stop by the Whistle Stop Café. Bring a camera if you're a *Fried Green Tomatoes* movie fan, and imagine yourself deep in the plot of amazing Southern food and hospitality.

CRISPY MATCHSTICK SWEET POTATO FRIES WITH CINNAMON SUGAR

1 gallon water

4 large sweet potatoes, peeled

½ cup kosher salt, plus more for sprinkling

2 quarts vegetable oil, divided

1 tablespoon ground cinnamon

2 tablespoons sugar

Pour the water into a large glass bowl. Cut the sweet potatoes lengthwise into ¼-inch slices. Stack four slices together, and slice into ¼-inch sticks. Add to the water, making sure they are all submerged. Stir in the salt and let the potatoes cure for 3 hours. Drain the potatoes and pat dry with paper towels.

Pour 1 quart of the oil into a deep saucepan and heat over medium to 220 degrees. Add 1 cup batches of the sweet potatoes to the simmering oil. Fry the potatoes for 2 minutes.

Remove the potatoes to a paper towel–lined plate to absorb the excess oil. Once all the potatoes have been fried, increase the oil temperature to 350 degrees and add the remaining quart of oil.

In small batches fry the potatoes again until crispy, 5 to 7 minutes.

Remove the fries from the oil, and drain on a paper towel–lined plate. Immediately season with the cinnamon, sugar, and additional salt. Serve immediately.

Serves 4 to 6.

KENTUCKY

When you bring up the state of Kentucky, most people think of one of three things: horse racing, bourbon, or the Colonel of Kentucky Fried Chicken. Having lived in the South for a while now, I'm still surprised that one of the most popular national fried chicken chains began in Kentucky, a border state that's a mix of North and South, with no definitive sway in one direction or the other. That being said, I found plenty of good Southern food along my travels in this state, and the state itself has plenty to share.

Kentucky is no stranger to conflict. Initially, the area was home to a large population of Native Americans from the tribes of the Shawnee, Cherokee, and Chickasaw. During the French and Indian War, exploration of the state by Europeans was put on hold due to vicious fighting. During the Civil War, brother often fought against brother due to strong divisions over slavery, despite the state's attempt at remaining neutral. Strangely enough, the two main leaders in the Civil War, Abraham Lincoln and Jefferson Davis, were both born in Kentucky, within one year and one hundred miles of each other.

Kentucky is composed of four major regions: western, south-central, north-central, and eastern. Each region has its own unique landscape and identity. As I traveled across the state, I was intrigued by each. The western region is known for bluegrass traditions and the beautiful Land Between the Lakes. The south-central region is known for its dozens of lakes and extensive cave systems unlike any other around the globe. In the north-central region, you will find rolling hills and Kentucky's claim to fame: horse country. The eastern region of the state is home to outdoor adventures with the Appalachian Mountains as the backdrop.

With its first permanent settlement established in 1774 at Fort Harrod and the Kentucky Derby a time-honored tradition since 1875, Kentucky is rich with history. And if you're looking for a good glass of bourbon to sip while watching a horse race, you've hit the jackpot. Kentucky really surprised me with its versatility.

The same could be said of the restaurants I visited in this state. With New Orleans Creole flavors from Gumbo Ya Ya's in Lexington to the full bourbon bar at the Harper

House in Hopkinsville, Kentucky definitely kept me on my toes in the hunt for the best Southern meat and three restaurants. Often I was put off of my usual game with amazing surprises such as a delicious all-you-can-eat mini buffet at the Downtown Diner in Henderson. Normally I not only would pass by this type of establishment but might even hit the gas pedal a little harder just to distance myself a little more quickly if possible. But my meal there was a welcome surprise of endless deliciousness.

And then there are places such as the Merrick Inn in Louisville, which has Southern food offerings in an old-school, upscale setting. The places I visited in Kentucky were all so unique and different that I never knew what to expect next. So if you're looking for a state that can offer you some tasty Southern food without making you feel stuck in a rut, Kentucky is a pretty safe bet. Just be sure to leave your preconceptions at the border, or you may miss out on some very tasty meals.

Gumbo Ya Ya's

Lexington, Kentucky

As soon as I decided to visit Gumbo Ya Ya's, I knew that I wasn't going to get original recipes. The classical form and family recipes that go into operating this type of establishment are seriously protected, and Gumbo Ya Ya's recipes are no exception. This restaurant menu is full of dishes that were developed over generations of testing to determine what tastes best and will keep the masses drooling.

Gumbo Ya Ya's was intriguing because as out of place as it seemed in Lexington, I felt right at home. Even from the parking lot, you can smell the flavors of New Orleans. As a young chef, I learned how to prepare a perfect roux. For those non-cooks out there, well, it's not easy, and I knew when I stepped out of the car, the roux was right at Gumbo Ya Ya's. A classic roux is the combination of fat and flour that's used as a thickening agent. Thinking back on the advent of the roux, I wonder who figured out how to use flour and fat to make such a stellar taste. When you cook it for extended periods of time, it begins to develop a nutty, rich aroma and flavor. It's the foundation for most thickened soups, gumbos, and stews in Creole cuisine. Pretty cool stuff, and to me it was even cooler that I stumbled into Gumbo Ya Ya's in Lexington. Would I be a fool not to try the gumbo at a restaurant called Gumbo Ya Ya's? The answer is yes. So first things first: gumbo, please.

As I marched my way through the menu, divided into small, medium, and large plates, I noticed one more Southern dish that gave me goosebumps. Maque Choux is a savory, sweet, almost pickled corn relish, and I couldn't pass it up. Inspired by Indian cuisine, it is a dish that Southerners have enjoyed for hundreds of years. It blurs the lines of seasonality and embraces everything you think of when preparing a menu based on local ingredients. Following is my recipe for the delicious Maque Choux. If you happen to be in Lexington and craving some Creole food, don't forget to stop by Gumbo Ya Ya's.

6 ounces salt pork, chopped into ½-inch pieces

½ cup vegetable oil

1 pound fresh okra, sliced ¼ inch thick

1 red bell pepper, chopped

1 yellow onion, finely chopped

2 teaspoons fresh thyme leaves

6 garlic cloves, minced

1 jalapeño pepper, minced

Pinch of cayenne pepper

2 teaspoons salt

5 cups corn kernels

1 cup heavy cream

2 green onions, thinly sliced

MAQUE CHOUX

Place the fatback in a large pan over medium heat and cook, stirring occasionally, until the fat is rendered. Using a spoon, transfer the fatback to a paper towel–lined plate to drain. Reserve the grease in the pan. Add the oil to the pan and increase the heat to high. Add the okra and cook, stirring occasionally, for 10 minutes. Remove the okra and reserve in a bowl. Reduce the heat to medium-low and add the bell pepper, onion, thyme, garlic, jalapeño, and cayenne. Cook, stirring occasionally, for about 5 minutes. Taste and add salt.

Add the corn and cook until the corn is crisp-tender, about 6 minutes. Add the cream and stir to incorporate. Add back the okra and cook until the cream is absorbed, about 3 minutes.

Remove the pan from the heat and add the green onions and reserved fatback. Stir until all the ingredients are well incorporated. Add salt and pepper to taste. Serve immediately.

Serves 6 to 8.

Home Café and Marketplace

Bowling Green, Kentucky

During my travels through Kentucky, I spent several days in Bowling Green, and I left nothing uneaten. The food memories are as strong as the memories I have of the people I encountered. Kentucky is famous for certain types of food—the Hot Brown, Derby Pie, and pecan pie—so I knew it would be tasty. The idea that I might stumble upon some hidden meat and three gems that really deserved my hungry attention excited me. That's just what happened at Home Café and Marketplace in Bowling Green.

The name leaves little to question about exactly what's happening here. The Home Café may feel like a home, but it's a full-fledged busy restaurant. The line I waited in at lunchtime was no joke. From the call-ahead orders, catering, and sit-down business, this place was booming. The story behind Home Café is very cool. In a nutshell, the business was born out of the inspiration of some classically trained chefs with a love for great food and an idea to make it available to everyone, all the time, and at fair prices. The dining room may be small and always full, but the counter-style service moved the pace quickly and made for a wonderful experience.

Best known for sandwiches and gourmet pizzas, the Home Café differs from more traditional Southern meat and threes, but it's the details within the details that I found when dining there that persuaded me to include the restaurant in this journey. There isn't a typical vegetable and meat menu that you would normally find at a Southern meat and three. The chefs determine the menu based on what's fresh and available locally.

Surprisingly, I passed on the fried green tomato pizza—I know, shame on me. However, what I encountered was a better choice for my list and a unique twist on a classic dish. "Summer in the South" is a plate lunch with house-made pimento cheese, fried green tomatoes, and strawberry preserves. Minding my manners, I delicately danced around my request for the pimento cheese recipe as I ate my lunch, while taking notice of all the flavors and textures. I assumed that I would be met with a definite no; they couldn't possibly share such a delicious recipe with me. Or could they? Amazingly and with pride, they did share the original recipe for the pimento cheese. And for fun, I've included my own strawberry preserve recipe. Now you too can dine like a king and enjoy the flavors from Home Café.

5 cups grated sharp Cheddar cheese, at room temperature

1 (8-ounce) package cream cheese, softened

1 cup mayonnaise

1 tablespoon grated yellow onion

1 teaspoon ground red pepper

1 (8-ounce) jar whole peeled pimientos, drained and diced

PIMENTO CHEESE

In a large bowl, mix together the grated cheese, cream cheese, mayonnaise, onion, and ground red pepper, stirring until blended but not smooth. Fold the pimientos into the mixture until it is blended and somewhat smooth.

Serves 8.

STRAWBERRY PRESERVES

2 quarts very ripe fresh
strawberries

6 cups sugar

½ cup fresh lemon juice

Wash and core the strawberries. Place them in a large saucepan and
cover with the sugar. Let stand for 3 hours.

Bring the strawberries and sugar to a boil over medium-high heat.
Add the lemon juice. Cook at a slow boil until the mixture becomes a
thick syrup, 12 to 15 minutes.

Pour the mixture into a shallow bowl and let stand until cooled;
cover and refrigerate for 24 hours.

Serves 12.

Lil Country Diner

Glasgow, Kentucky

Lil Country Diner is a small counter-service meat and three joint that feeds the little community of Glasgow. A memorial wall dedicated to the local men and women who have served in the military over the years is probably the largest and most unique memorial I've ever seen. The wall is peppered with pictures of the locals who served their country and paid the highest price. Although it has nothing to do with the restaurant business, or my search for the best meat and three joints all over the South, the wall and the humanity it portrayed speaks volumes about the kind of people who run Lil Country.

My love affair with Southern meat and three joints is based on the fact that they're real. They're centered on the concepts of inviting someone into your home and serving authentic food. The places that call themselves family-owned and -operated restaurants mean every word. From the welcome at the entrance to the aromas of the food to the locals catching up on the day's events, Southern meat and three restaurants feel exactly like home.

When you walk in the door of Lil Country, you are met with a steam table, counter service, and a menu board that changes daily and is filled with favorites and house specialties. Once I figured out what I wanted to eat, I was immediately put into a visually induced diabetic coma by the offering of luxurious pies, tarts, and puddings. There is certainly some

strategy to the dessert placement. It's right in your face, and before you have had a single bite, you start thinking about dessert.

My healthy-sized portions of food at the Lil Country Diner were all outstanding and familiar. My eyes are always bigger than my stomach, and when I chose the meatloaf, mashed potatoes, sweet potato fries, and pinto beans, I knew before I got the order out of my mouth I was in for a carbohydrate coma. The difficult aspects of eating and determining what would be considered the best isn't as easy as you think. Heavy is the Crown when eating your way around the South. Each of the flavors were exactly what I assumed they would be: well seasoned, well thought, and well executed. But those beans . . . they weren't just pinto beans, because I've tasted my weight in beans and these were beans from the heavens. The experience would lead me back to the diner as a regular without a doubt. I stumbled through Kentucky eating everything from gourmet pizza to drinking bathtubs full of sweet tea, but the most remarkable little gem at Lil Country came in the form of a legume. The Lil Country Diner and those tasty little pinto beans were the hook in the whole story. Like the plot of a soap opera that pulls you in right before the commercial break, my hook was the pinto beans. Yours may be different; however, the first step will be making this local joint a must-see on your road trip of Southern food.

2 cups dry pinto beans

3 ounces salt pork

2 teaspoons salt

Freshly cracked black pepper

PINTO BEANS

Rinse the beans thoroughly to remove any debris. Place the beans in a large bowl, and cover with tap water. Cover the bowl with plastic wrap, and soak the beans in the refrigerator for 24 hours.

When you remove the beans to cook, most of the water should have been absorbed. Drain the remaining water and give the beans a quick rinse to remove any debris or excess starchiness. Fill a large pot with water and add the salt pork. Bring to a full boil over high heat. Drain the beans and add them to the pan. Add the salt and pepper. Reduce the heat to medium or medium-low and cook the beans for 3 hours.

Serves 4 to 6.

NOTE: The Lil Country Diner serves these beans with warm cornbread and chilled butter.

Lisa's 5th Street Diner

Bowling Green, Kentucky

When I travel, I like playing a game to discover what the locals think is the best place in town. I'm not eating a meal until I can get several locals to suggest the same location at least three times. The game works well, unless I'm starving and irritable. Bowling Green is the perfect location for my game, because the restaurant scene outside of the college campus area is a little sparse, and frankly, I was hungry enough to really tear into a meal. The consensus on the restaurant tip of the day was Lisa's 5th Street Diner.

Bowling Green has a population of about sixty thousand people. It's the state's the third largest city. Although it's home to the state's largest public university (Western Kentucky University), manufacturing companies such as General Motors and Fruit of the Loom, and a serious group of Corvette enthusiasts and the corvette museum, it feels like a small country town.

When I eat at a restaurant for the first time, I try to enjoy my experience just as the owners have created it. Since I'm from the restaurant industry, sometimes I overthink the process, especially if I'm famished. So there I was at Lisa's 5th Street Diner, ruminating about the restaurant's name. After all, it's on Center Street, not 5th Street, but once I entered the restaurant, thoughts about the misnomer disappeared. The locals recommended Lisa's for a "big boy" Kentucky breakfast. But this is a big boy breakfast with a twist. I noticed fried cabbage on the menu, and I liked the way that

sounded. Fried vegetables are really the secret key to my heart.

After I ordered, a brigade of well-oiled staff members began to deliver my meal. I only ordered one meal; however, the portions are so generous that it required several servers to quickly swoop in and drop my four separate plates. I played it safe to some extent, pulling a mulligan if you will. I ordered pancakes, scrambled eggs, potatoes, sausage with a few biscuits and a side of gravy, and, oh yeah, my side of fried cabbage. I'm a food-goober, because after I ordered this enormous breakfast in the middle of the day and added the cabbage as a side, I immediately texted a few chef friends to tell them I was eating fried cabbage for lunch—"in your face!"

The service at Lisa's 5th Street Diner makes you feel at home. I became part of the conversation organically, as the staff hollered across the restaurant. It was quite efficient and saved many steps. There was no show being put on at Lisa's. It was just real, good, honest people, cooking incredible Southern food. For the breakfast I ordered, the portions exceeded the space in my belly, no matter how empty it felt, but I saved room for my fried cabbage. And just as I thought, the delicious, tender texture of the cabbage was accentuated by the gentle pan fry—part earthy and part indulgent. There were no frills, just fresh cabbage turned into a fun Southern side that saved me from blazing through a fast-food chain.

2 quarts water

Salt

1 head green cabbage

½ cup (1 stick) butter

3 tablespoons vegetable oil
or shortening

Pepper to taste

Pinch of sugar

Splash of vinegar

FRIED CABBAGE

Pour the water into a large pot and bring to a full boil over high heat. Generously season with salt.

Cut the cabbage into halves and remove the core. Cube the cabbage leaves into 1-inch squares and submerge them in the boiling water. Blanch for 3 to 4 minutes. Transfer the cabbage to a colander to drain.

In a large sauté pan over medium-high heat, add the butter and oil. Add the cabbage and fry, stirring occasionally, until browned and wilted, 8 to 10 minutes. Season the cabbage with additional salt and add pepper to taste. Add the sugar and vinegar and cook until the vinegar has evaporated, about 3 minutes. Stir well to incorporate the flavors, and serve.

Serves 6.

Mark's Feed Store

Louisville, Kentucky

enjoy Louisville, but I think I may like potato salad more. That may sound strange; however, the combination of perfectly cooked, seasoned potatoes doused in an elaborate mayonnaise, well, I think that sounds pretty darn good. When I first thought about discovering and sharing all types of Southern foods, I saw potato salad as almost a supporting role to the other lead edible characters. But this is a really unfair assignment to the potato salad. If you ask any Southerner what types of dishes you may find on the typical supper table, I'm almost sure ten out of ten will answer potato salad. It's timeless and can be reinvented as often as you like, or not at all, if you're holding on to a great recipe such as the one at Mark's Feed Store in Louisville. This popular five-restaurant chain found success in the mid-1980s. Since then, it has been serving Kentucky and Indiana real barbecue and meat and three plates that capture the essence of Southern food.

In the past when I've traveled through Kentucky, I've been enamored with the ideas of an authentic hot brown or a huge helping of burgoo, but during this trip the potato salad completely captivated me.

The restaurant I chose was the location in the Highlands on Bardstown Road, where the reclaimed building provides the perfect backdrop. The menu at Mark's boasts a variety of items. The restaurant was conceived on barbecue, but between the daily specials and the combinations, the entire roster for a typical meat and three is covered.

The food at Mark's is amazing, but it wasn't the barbecue that stole my heart. Surprisingly, it was the potato salad. It's a stand-alone type of potato salad that can complement any entrée or step up and capture the lead role. Here is the recipe from the original Mark's.

RED POTATO SALAD

4 pounds red potatoes, unpeeled, quartered

5 large eggs

2 cups mayonnaise

4 tablespoons heavy cream

3 tablespoons white vinegar

1 cup minced green onions

1 teaspoon salt

½ teaspoon pepper

1 ½ cups minced celery

Bring a large pot of salted water to a full boil over high heat. Add the potatoes and cook until tender but firm, 12 to 15 minutes. Drain, let cool, and then dice into 1-inch cubes.

Place the eggs in a saucepan and cover with cool water. Bring the water to a full boil over high heat and cook for 2 minutes. Remove the pan from the heat and cover the pan. Let stand for 12 minutes. Place the eggs in a bowl of cold water and let cool, then peel and chop.

In a chilled glass or metal bowl whisk together the mayonnaise, heavy cream, vinegar, green onions, salt, and pepper. Add the potatoes and stir well to coat all the potatoes. Fold in the eggs and celery. Refrigerate 2 to 3 hours before serving.

Serves 12.

The Merrick Inn

Louisville, Kentucky

The Merrick Inn in Louisville has been the epitome of Southern food for decades. The space was originally designed as a stable and housed award-winning racehorses. As the home to the Kentucky Derby at Churchill Downs, often called "the most exciting two minutes in sports," the city and its culture center around horse racing. Each year since 1875, the Derby boasts not only a growing number of spectators to the sport but a high stakes race for the country's best racehorses. Now we get to the food of the Derby—mint juleps, bowls of thick Kentucky burgoo, or possibly the classic hot brown. These culinary gems have helped define the food around the Derby and have been as much a tradition as "The Run for the Roses." The race may be only two minutes, but the city shuts down for weeks to celebrate the upcoming race.

The Merrick Inn thrives during Derby season. The Murray family has owned and operated the Merrick Inn since the early 1970s, creating an atmosphere that embraces the total experience of Southern food and charm. I'm not sure I'd classify this restaurant as a "joint" but more of an occasion and a place to enjoy a superb Southern supper. The red carpet is rolled out each day, and the combination of skill, service, and quality shine through to enhance each guest's experience. The Merrick Inn focuses its attention on daily menus. There is, however, a standard menu that locals gush over if you ask them about their favorite place in town to enjoy classic Southern fare.

The decor at the Merrick Inn could be best described as Commander's Palace meets Cracker Barrel, and I mean that in the best way possible. The comfortable, relaxed atmosphere feels like home, but the elegance makes guests who choose the Inn as a dining option feel rewarded.

The choice for my outstanding meal at this location and the item that most represents the restaurant, Southern food, and Kentucky is the Merrick Inn's delicious prime rib of beef. Too often restaurants will offer prime rib with the mindset that roasting a rib of beef heavily coated in salt and pepper is prime rib. Ehh, no. That couldn't be further from the reality of what a prime rib of beef should be. The real process is long and involves controlling temperatures for extended periods of time. Imagine trying to cook a piece of meat for four to six hours while keeping the required internal temperature somewhere in the range of rare. Sounds almost impossible, right? Well it isn't easy. At the Merrick Inn, the prime rib is what you would expect from a multi-starred steakhouse, a restaurant whose entire existence is centered on cooking meat.

The small, family-owned, multi-generation Southern eatery, with the practice of over forty years, excels at prime rib. Imagine your meaty dreams coming true. I knew I wanted the rib, but with as much care as they invest into the meat cooking they also don't hold back on the sides. The prime rib was elevated with roasted vegetable ragout and cloud-like mashed potatoes. I particularly enjoyed the sliced local tomato with a touch of salt. It wins my heart every time. I know you will enjoy this recipe, and when you're in Louisville, stop by the Merrick Inn for a time-tested taste of the real thing that's sure to place first.

PRIME RIB AU JUS

For the prime rib, rinse the beef in cool water and pat dry.

Combine the salt, pepper, minced garlic, and oil in a small bowl until it becomes a paste. Massage the paste into the roast. Place the beef on a large plate, cover, and refrigerate for 1 hour.

Preheat the oven to 200 degrees.

Place the roast on a rack over a deep roasting pan. Cook, uncovered, for 4 to 6 hours, until the center reaches 120 degrees on a meat thermometer. Allow the meat to rest for 30 minutes before slicing.

For the jus, bring the contents of the roasting pan to a simmer over medium heat. This will be some meat and mostly fat. Add the beef stock, red wine, salt, and pepper and cook until reduced by half. Remove the pan from the heat and whisk in the chilled butter until the sauce has thickened. Place the jus in a serving bowl and serve alongside the sliced prime rib.

Serves 12.

Prime Rib

1 (6- to 8-pound) beef rib roast

4 tablespoons kosher salt

2 teaspoons freshly cracked black pepper

6 cloves garlic, minced

2 tablespoons vegetable oil

Jus

4 cups beef stock

1 cup dry red wine

1 teaspoon kosher salt, plus more as needed

1 teaspoon freshly cracked black pepper, plus more as needed

2 tablespoons cold butter

The Café at Louisville Antique Mall

Louisville, Kentucky

A café nestled in the middle of a mall full of antiques, well, it's a good idea. All over the South there are tiny little antique malls with even smaller cafés. The small eateries often fly under the radar until they develop a local following that includes more than the shoppers and antique scavengers. Sal and Cindy Rubino of the Café at Louisville Antique Mall are no strangers to the restaurant business. In fact, with multiple success stories under their belt, they saw a huge opportunity at the Antique Mall and grabbed it. The foundation of this café is as Southern and magnificent as possible. Well-known in the area for having a remarkable breakfast, the café goes a step further with daily plate lunches and signature menu items that will bring you to the mall for more than a collection of rare doilies.

Running a breakfast restaurant takes a true commitment from the owners and staff. Waking up each morning and heading into work to cook for others requires a sense of serving, hospitality, and love for food and people. While that message often gets lost in a lot of noise surrounding chefs, the food and beverage industry as a whole is truly rooted in giving. I found that hospitality and wonderful giving nature during my visit to the Café. It wasn't just the interaction with the staff; it was the entire picture. Nestled in a restored historic building, the café has developed a following, and I witnessed residents of the Louisville Highlands neighborhood arrive to pick up their grab-and-go orders while I waited for my breakfast. It's a natural fit and an organic hotspot serving the community with love.

The food at the Louisville Café is perfectly executed—from the Grit Scramble, to the pimento cheese sandwich, to the signature specialties such as the Art Deco (an elevated version of the BLT with peppery guacamole). The details at the Café come together so well—the atmosphere, the service, the menu and daily specials, the customer feedback in the community, and the owners' approach to the business, and how they represent themselves day to day. None of these qualities is over-thought. They just happen, because the Café is run by honest, hardworking folks who want to take care of the people who take care of them.

At the Café in the Antique Mall that's exactly what Sal and Cindy Rubino have been doing for years. As their business grows, so will the community. It's an ideal business plan: make one person happy and satisfied, and they will share their experience with everyone.

The detail I found most amazing, believe it or not, was the sweet tea. You might think that sweet tea is just a grace note on the menu, but if you ask any owner of a Southern joint to name one of the most important elements of what makes them who they are, the answer will often be the sweet tea. Prepared by the bathtub load, the sweet tea at the café is serious. It's just sweet enough, but with tea that tastes like tea—not tea-flavored water with syrup. Sweet tea, in my experience, is regionally different. In Mississippi it's typically a bit sweeter, while in Tennessee it's slightly more diluted. In Alabama it's sometimes sweeter and stronger, while in Florida the tea is more of the sun tea version. Enjoy this original recipe. Make it at home often, and when you feel the overwhelming euphoria while sipping a glass, you will learn an important secret: it's the insane amount of sugar and caffeine that keeps the South moving.

2 cups sugar

11 cups water, divided

4 orange pekoe family-size tea bags

16 large ice cubes

SWEET TEA

Add the sugar to a large pitcher. Pour 8 cups water into a medium saucepan and bring to a boil over high heat. Remove the pan from the heat and add the tea bags. Let the bags steep in the hot water for 5 to 7 minutes.

Remove the tea bags and pour the warm tea over the sugar in the pitcher. Stir until the sugar is fully dissolved. Add the remaining 3 cups of cold water and ice cubes. Stir the tea and let the ice melt. Taste the tea. If it's too bitter or over sweetened, add additional water, 1 cup at a time, to dilute.

Serves 6 to 8.

The Downtown Diner

Henderson, Kentucky

The Downtown Diner … downtown where? Henderson, Kentucky, to be exact, is where I found my next meal, and I can't wait to share the original recipe I enjoyed there and the stories behind such a wonderful little gem.

I usually avoid the all-you-can-eat establishments. Sometimes the food is lacking in quality and trying to make up for it in quantity. In this case, though, I was proven a fool. The Downtown Diner was about all I can eat; however, the food was so amazing and well prepared I didn't need to or want to overeat and maximize my dollar. I found myself sampling the offerings, tasting and noticing the real, big flavors and how they chose fresh ingredients.

Here are their keys to success: first, the menu changes every day, and, second, the Downtown Diner only serves breakfast and lunch, so the offerings are limited and focused. I spoke with a dozen of the regulars inside the restaurant and on the streets leading up to my visit, and they all had their favorite offerings. Henderson is small, but not so small that there are limited dining options. The locals choose to support this restaurant and crave breakfast and lunch from the little joint. The diner is pictured in almost every town photo because of its strategic location. Henderson has a population of almost thirty thousand people, and my bet is that most of the inhabitants are regular customers at the Downtown Diner. The dining area hums with the conversation of folks with big personalities, and I left wishing I was a fly on the wall during business hours on most days. The locals congregate and share the day's happenings, and as a tourist, one can't help but eavesdrop.

The diner's play list of tasty meals has as much to offer as you would expect from a larger city's restaurant. I noshed on a little of everything, and my dining companion ate as though it was his last meal. The Manhattan Steak curiously intrigued me. The flavors were deep, mysterious, and delicious. The braised, crock-pot style beef comes together effortlessly, and unless you really screw up, it's a very consistent recipe to add to your recipe repertoire. It was the most unique and flavorful of what I enjoyed. It was also the feature of the day and satisfied all the savory, spicy, and sweet moments I was looking for.

MANHATTAN BEEF

5 pounds rump roast

4 tablespoons salt

2 tablespoons freshly cracked black pepper

½ cup ketchup

2 quarts water

1 large yellow onion, minced

2 teaspoons garlic powder

1 teaspoon chili powder

2 tablespoons Worcestershire sauce

1 cup all-purpose flour

Season the meat with salt and pepper. Slather the ketchup on the roast and rub into all sides. Place the roast on a large plate, cover, and refrigerate for 1 hour.

Preheat the oven to 375 degrees.

Place the roast on the rack of a roasting pan and cover. Bake for 3 to 4 hours, until tender. Transfer the roast to a cutting board to rest. Strain the broth and drippings from the roasting pan into a large saucepan and add 2 quarts of water. Bring to a full boil over high heat. Add the onions, garlic powder, chili powder, and Worcestershire sauce. Cook until the mixture is reduced by half, then whisk in the flour to thicken.

When the meat is cool, slice and serve with the pan gravy.

Serves 10 to 12.

Harper House

Hopkinsville, Kentucky

Are you making plans for a trip to Hopkinsville? After enjoying the feast that the Daniels family created at Harper House, I'm looking for rentals in town. Husband and wife Chris and Nelson Daniels wanted a place of their own, and Hopkinsville needed a new restaurant. So in 2009, with quality, style, and tastes of the familiar, the Daniels launched Harper House, an eatery that projects just enough attitude to wake up the sleepy palate of Hopkinsville. Successful restaurants attract a new group of customers who eat out often, while taking care not to intimidate the existing clientele. The Harper House has done this perfectly.

Noticing the tastefully restored and recovered material used to construct the building and space leads me to believe that my dining experience will not fall short on delicious details. The restaurant is a striking combination of a posh meat and three and an upscale bistro. The food and menu reflect the area, and the ingredients are Southern, local, and timeless. Harper House is one of the few joints on my journey that boasts a full bar. It offers a bourbon selection that leaves every pairing covered. The menu includes maple bacon Brussels sprouts, smoked Gouda mac 'n' cheese, hash brown casserole, steak burgers, meatloaf, and the most velvety memorable mashed potatoes I've ever encountered (well, except my own, of course). You can get lost quickly in all the offerings at the Harper House. The service matches the menu and the atmosphere. I think that is what really defines a successful eatery, no matter how small or large, old or new. If the concept offers a feeling of togetherness, and service is as good as the food, then the rest falls into place effortlessly. It's a winner.

At Harper House, I skipped dessert and went straight for another course of mashed potatoes. I can try to describe the magical texture and how the buttery potatoes felt, tasted, and settled in my mouth, but I couldn't do them justice. Instead, I'll share my recipe of this stellar mashed potato memory. It won't be a memory for long because if I have it my way, the Daniels family will either hire me or let me move in upstairs so I'm one step closer to the real Harper House recipe.

6 large russet potatoes, peeled and cubed

3 quarts cold water

Kosher salt to taste

8 cloves garlic, peeled

½ quart heavy cream

1 cup (2 sticks) butter, chilled and divided

White pepper to taste

ROASTED GARLIC MASHED POTATOES

Preheat the oven to 350 degrees.

Place the potatoes in a large pot and add the cold water. Add a pinch of salt and bring to a boil over high heat. Cook until the potatoes are fork tender but not falling apart, about 20 minutes.

While the potatoes are cooking, place the garlic cloves on a baking sheet and roast for 15 to 20 minutes, until golden brown.

Pour the potatoes into a strainer and place the empty pot back on the stove. Add the heavy cream and 1 stick of the butter to the pot. Heat over medium-high heat until the mixture begins to simmer.

Once the potatoes have drained and while they are still warm, add them to the cream mixture. Simmer 10 minutes.

Pour the potatoes and cream into a large mixing bowl. Using an electric mixer with a wire whisk, beat the potatoes on low speed until they are thick and creamy like peanut butter. Smash the garlic and add it to the bowl. Continue to mix on low until the mixture becomes fully incorporated, 5 to 7 minutes.

Season with white pepper and salt, as desired. Transfer the potatoes to a serving bowl. Cube the remaining 1 stick of cold butter, and slowly fold it into the potatoes until it has melted and created a soft, velvety consistency. Check the seasoning and reseason if needed.

Serves 6 to 8.

Two Rivers Restaurant

Carrollton, Kentucky

This is a first for me: a restaurant that's on the property of a state park. The location was a perfect place for me to make a pit stop. On a trip from Memphis to Cincinnati, I needed hot food and a break from the road. Where the Ohio and the Kentucky rivers meet, I found the Two Rivers Restaurant, a charming little eatery that serves hundreds of wonderful Southern meals each day. The scenery is amazing. As I stepped away from the breathtaking view, wishing I had grabbed a camera, I was drawn into the enormous lodge-looking structure. The entrance leads you into a giant room that is full of hungry travelers and customers who can't get enough of the nine-dollar meals.

The restaurant is part cafeteria and part buffet, with lots of Southern hospitality. The portions are massive and waist-altering, and if you clear your plate you should feel bad about yourself and immediately go for a hike.

The restaurant is a new addition and a welcomed one for both locals and park guests. It's owned and operated by the State of Kentucky and the Kentucky Department of Parks. They designed the space with locals in mind, selecting items for the decor that are regionally relevant and putting together a menu that honors many of the farmers and producers in the region. The business is thriving with the recent changes to the landscape and concept, and sales were nearly 30 percent higher this year than the previous.

I was originally hooked on getting the recipe for Two Rivers' pancakes, because they're silly good. But when I tasted the country ham, I reconsidered. The Kentucky cured ham is like Benton ham in Tennessee. It's the embodiment of what's happening in the food scene in the region. Its incredible quality mirrors the concept the state has put forward at Two Rivers Restaurant, and it shows visitors what Kentucky is all about. It's about serious food—food that speaks of the South while representing the state and each individual local market. It's fun food that is Southern, but with slight Northern influences and creative touches. That's what's best about taking note of food regionally. Although it may be slightly different, it's never so different that you can't appreciate the labor of love.

I'd make a trip again to Kentucky just for the view of the two rivers colliding and the stacks upon stacks of pancake goodness. The atmosphere is fun, regionally respectful, and makes you feel that you are exactly where you need to be—in a park cabin crushing tasty food.

The recipe I've selected to represent this joint is something I will call my own—the Penn Cured Country Ham. It will call you to Kentucky to taste what I've experienced. I've added some red-eye gravy to help you stay awake on your travels.

1 (6-ounce) country ham steak

½ teaspoon all-purpose flour

1 cup brewed black coffee

2 tablespoons butter

Pinch of salt and pepper

Dash of your favorite hot sauce

1 teaspoon brown sugar

PENN CURED COUNTRY HAM WITH RED-EYE GRAVY

In a large cast-iron skillet over medium-high heat, cook the ham steak until browned on both sides, 6 to 8 minutes. Remove the steak to a plate and stir the flour into the drippings and ham pieces left in the pan. Add the coffee and whisk to thicken the gravy. Add the butter, salt, pepper, and hot sauce and whisk until incorporated. Add the brown sugar and whisk until the sugar dissolves and the mixture begins to bubble. Taste for accuracy, reseason if necessary, and add more hot sauce if you're brave. Serve the gravy alongside the ham or pour over the top.

Serves 1 to 2.

NOTE: Two Rivers Restaurant serves Penn Hams brand.

LOUISIANA

Two things come to mind when most people think of Louisiana: Bourbon Street in New Orleans and the chaos that is known as Mardi Gras. But Louisiana is so much more than a single street or event. The people of this state have a culture all their own, complete with music, food, and even a way of speaking that is unlike any other in this nation.

The people of Louisiana also know how to take their time and never shy away from a fight. I love the history of this state, with all its twists and turns. One of my favorite historical facts about Louisiana is that the Battle of New Orleans, where future president Andrew Jackson gained his notoriety, was actually fought two weeks after the War of 1812 was over. The news of the war's end didn't reach the state in time to call off the battle. Talk about digging in and carrying on—that's what these people are known for.

Although Louisiana has a population of diverse cultural backgrounds, two prominent ethnic groups comprise most of the population—the Cajuns and the Creoles. Cajuns are descendants of a French-speaking group of Acadians from Canada. Creoles are people with a mixed French, Spanish, Caribbean, African, and Native American background. The people in Louisiana are all about flavor, not just in their food but also in their way of life. As I traveled throughout the state, I met people determined to get every bit of spice out of life. Louisianans aren't just characters, they also have character. Just look at the list of people who came from Louisiana—Louis Armstrong, Truman Capote, and Fats Domino, just to name a few.

The vibrancy of the state carries far from the port of New Orleans, all the way to the state borders. From the memories of the charismatic Lea Johnson, a restaurant owner in Lecompte, stealing the *Tonight Show* spotlight from Johnny Carson, to the sisters Angela and Tina carrying on their father's dreams at Lasyone's Meat Pie Restaurant, there are great stories and good food just around every corner of this state. So the next time you think about taking a trip down to Louisiana, don't wait until Fat Tuesday and miss out on the good food and good times you can have the rest of the year. Follow my lead and get off the beaten path. You will experience just as much flavor as you can handle.

Aunt Ellie's

Lutcher, Louisiana

When you travel as much as I do, you take comfort in the small things that make a place feel like home, and Aunt Ellie's in Lutcher is a great place to find comfort. The building itself doesn't speak much to the homey feel, with its cold aluminum siding, but when you get inside, you want to relax and stay awhile.

Inside, a mural depicts an old-timey kitchen complete with a pie cooling on the windowsill. The dining room is small, but cozy. Vinyl tablecloths cover the tables, and the latticework separating the dining room from the kitchen adds a nice touch.

The menu offers several fried seafood options, burgers, salads, soups, and sandwiches. There is also a variety of daily specials. As I looked over the menu, I was drawn away from a typical plate lunch to the sandwich portion of the menu. I am somewhat of a BLT connoisseur. It's a simple sandwich combo of bacon, lettuce, and tomato, but executed perfectly, it can be a game changer. I decided to order the "Not Your Everyday BLT," with a cup of baked potato cheese soup to make it a meal. When my lunch arrived, the sandwich was great, and I can't say I was surprised. However, I was completely caught off guard by the way the simple cup of soup I had chosen stole the spotlight. The soup was thick and creamy with bits of bacon, cheese, and chives on the top. The potatoes were cooked well, with nice big chunks throughout the soup, and provided the creamy undertone that carried the weight of the dish. There was a delicate balance of cream, cheese, salt, and pepper that gave me a warm and fuzzy feeling inside. I fully expected to be writing this story about the BLT, but it was the unassuming cup of soup that grabbed my attention and made me feel at home.

My recipe on the following page is designed to bring you that same warm and fuzzy feeling I got that day. Please share the warmth with others. And if you're in Lutcher and feeling a little homesick, stop by Aunt Ellie's to be reminded of home.

Baked Potato Cheese Soup (page 108)

BAKED POTATO CHEESE SOUP

6 slices bacon, diced

4 tablespoons butter, chilled

½ cup all-purpose flour

4 cups milk, plus more as needed

3 russet potatoes, peeled and diced

2 yellow onions, sliced

1 ½ cup shredded Cheddar cheese, plus more for topping

1 cup sour cream

Kosher salt and freshly cracked black pepper to taste

Chopped green onions

Heat a large skillet over medium-high heat, add the bacon, and cook until brown and crispy. Transfer to a paper towel–lined plate to drain and cool. Crumble the bacon.

Melt the butter in a large pot or Dutch oven over medium heat. Whisk in the flour and cook until lightly browned. Whisk in the milk and cook, whisking constantly, until slightly thickened, about 2 minutes. Stir in the potatoes and onions. Bring to a boil, then reduce the heat to medium. Cook until potatoes are tender, 15 to 20 minutes. Stir in the cheese, sour cream, salt, and pepper. Serve immediately, with green onions, additional cheese, and the crumbled bacon.

Serves 4.

Bernard Cajun Sea-Fry Restaurant

Cottonport, Louisiana

One thing I've learned to appreciate about meat and three restaurants is their air of confidence. There is something to be said for a person or a place that exudes the spirit of being true to oneself without caring what anyone else thinks. That is exactly the feeling I got when I walked into Bernard Cajun Sea-Fry Restaurant in Cottonport.

The restaurant has a small, open dining room complete with about a dozen rectangular tables covered in red-and-white checkered vinyl tablecloths and mismatched chairs. As I spied a refrigerator sitting in the dining room, I thought, "These people know exactly who they are and don't care what anyone else thinks." It's refreshing. There is a significant difference between confidence and arrogance, and these people seem to get that.

This joint offers plate lunch specials Monday through Friday, but I was in the mood for something a little different than a typical meat and three meal. I was drawn to the po' boy section of the menu and reminded myself that I am in Louisiana, the birthplace of the po' boy.

After considering the selection of po' boys with everything from catfish to rib-eye steak, I decided to take the classic route and go for the shrimp po' boy. These sandwiches are traditionally served on a baguette and topped off with lettuce, tomato, and mayonnaise. I decided to forgo the cheese option, staying a purist through and through.

When my meal arrived, I knew I'd made the right choice. The bread had a crispy outer crust with light and fluffy goodness in the center. The shrimp were fried to a golden brown and spilled out over the sides of the bread. The batter was the perfect mix of salt, pepper, and that Creole kick I was hoping for. I devoured the sandwich in no time flat.

After returning home, I found myself craving the crunchy goodness of the po' boy I had while traipsing around the state of Louisiana, so I decided to recreate the delicious sandwich for myself. Enjoy the following recipe for a show-stopping sandwich when your usual cold cuts just aren't cutting it anymore. And when you need a breath of fresh air sprinkled with confidence, head on down to Cottonport, and drop by the Bernard Cajun Sea-Fry Restaurant.

SHRIMP PO' BOY

In a small bowl combine the mayonnaise, ketchup, horseradish sauce, Creole seasoning, garlic powder, paprika, and lemon juice and whisk until smooth. Refrigerate until ready to serve.

In a large cast-iron skillet over medium heat, add the butter and garlic. When the butter is melted, add the shrimp. Dust evenly with the Creole seasoning and cook the shrimp until pink all the way through. Remove the shrimp from the pan into a bowl.

Split the rolls in half and smear the remoulade inside each roll. Fill with shrimp and the garlic-butter mixture and top with cabbage, lemon juice, and additional remoulade.

Serves 4.

Remoulade

1 cup mayonnaise

2/3 cup ketchup

4 tablespoons horseradish sauce

1 tablespoon Creole seasoning

1 teaspoon garlic powder

1 teaspoon paprika

1 tablespoon lemon juice

Shrimp

6 tablespoons butter

2 tablespoons minced garlic

1 pound (16- to 20-count) peeled and deveined shrimp

1 teaspoon Creole seasoning

4 white crusty sandwich rolls

1 cup shredded cabbage

¼ teaspoon lemon juice

Blue Light Café

Ruston, Louisiana

Traveling around the South sampling the fare at local meat and three restaurants, I've noticed similarities, from the simple buildings, to the decor inside, to the menus. That's why the Blue Light Café in Ruston stands out so clearly in my mind. The restaurant is in an old house with lots of odd roof angles and aluminum siding. It's not your typical country cooking exterior.

The menu is posted on the wall with the selections changing daily. The restaurant is run by a group of older women—all very sweet and friendly. The counter service is a bit unusual. Customers write down their own menu selections, drink order, and table number and then take a seat.

The food is well known around these parts, and the fried pork chop has a somewhat legendary status. It's served on its own plate, with the sides dished up on a separate platter; there's just no room next to that behemoth of a chop. I was intrigued by the apparent "tall tales" of the locals and had to see that bad boy for myself.

I ordered the fried pork chop with mustard greens, mashed potatoes, and pinto beans. The chop was great—with super crispy breading while still moist and tender inside. Despite its grand appearance, it didn't steal my heart in this meal. The winner of that award was the simply prepared mustard greens. For those of you not familiar with mustard greens, they are similar to turnip greens, but with a slightly peppery flavor in contrast to the earthiness of turnip greens. The mustard greens at the Blue Light Café were amazing—tender and peppery with just the right amount of seasoning. I enjoyed them so much I've decided to share my recipe with you so that you too can experience the power of greens. And if you happen to be in Ruston anytime soon, don't hesitate to pull into the Blue Light Café and gawk at the mammoth fried pork chop while chowing down on some tasty eats.

MUSTARD GREENS

Place the butter in a large skillet over medium-high heat. Once the butter has melted, add the bacon and cook until crispy and translucent. Add the shallots and cook for 5 to 7 minutes longer. Add the mustard greens and cook, covered, for 30 minutes. Add the water, sugar, and a light sprinkling of salt and pepper, and stir until well mixed. Cover and cook, stirring occasionally, until the greens are tender, 15 to 20 minutes. Uncover, stir in the vinegar and red pepper flakes, reduce the heat to medium, and cook until the liquid is reduced by half. Add more salt and pepper as desired

Serves 10.

4 tablespoons butter

2 cups cubed smoked slab bacon

2 large shallots, minced

1 pound mustard greens, stems removed, chopped

½ gallon water

3 teaspoons sugar

Salt and pepper to taste

2 tablespoons champagne vinegar

1 teaspoon crushed red pepper flakes

Rocky & Carlo's Restaurant and Bar

Chalmette, Louisiana

With a remarkably thick Italian accent, Tommy Tommaseo is the least likely suspect I thought I'd find cooking remarkable Southern food. Tommy is the character shuffling through the kitchen at the iconic Rocky & Carlo's Restaurant and Bar in Chalmette. He is the mastermind behind the restaurant's popular macaroni and cheese. I have always thought certain dishes should never be promoted past a supporting role. One dish I put in that category is macaroni and cheese. Occasionally someone changes the pasta type around or puts in a variety of different cheeses, but the result is never enough for it to get top billing.

As I visited with Tommy, I learned that he has been making mac 'n' cheese for forty-eight years. The secret, he revealed, is "not too cook too much, but just enough." He explained that his customers like the dish all different ways: "Some like the bottom, some like the top, some like it with red gravy, and some like it with brown gravy." To Tommy, what matters is that he makes people happy. And he did just that for me, when he gave me his delicious recipe for mac 'n' cheese.

I tried to hold on to my preconceived notions, but I felt them slipping away. My first line of defense, my nose, couldn't contradict that there was something good happening here. Before I got too close to the intoxicating scent that was emanating from the kitchen, my eyes gave further evidence to my underestimating this satisfying comfort food. Ten minutes later, as my eight-dollar large plate was placed in front of me, I had to admit defeat.

ROCKY AND CARLO'S MAC 'N' CHEESE

Preheat the oven to 350 degrees.

Bring a large pot of water to a full boil over high heat. Liberally season the water with salt and add the macaroni. Cover and boil for about 10 minutes.

Drain the pasta and return it to the pan. Stir in butter cubes, eggs, half-and-half, salt, pepper, olive oil, and sharp Cheddar cheese until creamy. Taste and add additional salt and pepper, if needed. Pour into 3 or 4 pans. Sprinkle the mild Cheddar cheese over the macaroni.

Cover the pans with aluminum foil and bake for 45 minutes. Remove the foil and continuing baking for 30 minutes, or until browned. Let stand for 15 minutes before serving.

Serves 16 to 20.

NOTE: You can substitute rigatoni for the Maltagliati macaroni if you can't find it at your local grocery store.

2 pounds Maltagliati macaroni

½ cup (1 stick) butter, cubed

6 large eggs

2 cups half-and-half

2 teaspoons sea salt, plus more for salting water

2 teaspoons coarsely ground white pepper

2 teaspoons olive oil

4 cups shredded sharp Cheddar cheese

4 cups shredded mild Cheddar cheese

C-Bo's Country Kitchen

Winnfield, Louisiana

Known as a "Sportsman's Paradise," Winn Parish has beautiful natural settings, and the town of Winnfield is just one of its prime sites. I'm not much of a sportsman myself, but I can still appreciate the outdoor beauty of the area. When you're in an area that's a haven for hunters in the South, you know there will be a restaurant serving some tasty, satisfying food to fuel them for their long hours spent trekking through the woods. C-Bo's Country Kitchen in Winnfield is here to meet just that need.

C-Bo's is a simple place run by down-home country folk who just want to give people a good meal. They are well known among the locals for their barbecue and delicious cooking. Out back stands a giant barbecue smoker large enough to fit a whole hog. Inside, the dining room is simple with white painted brick walls and sparse decor. The focus here is on the flavors coming out of the kitchen, not the frivolities.

The restaurant offers daily specials of a few meats and a handful of fresh veggies to choose from as sides. But it was the sweet treats—home-baked pies and cakes perched on old-school glass cake pedestals I remember from my grandmother's house as a young boy—that caught my eye as I walked in.

I ordered chicken and dumplings with fried okra, purple hull peas, and snap beans. The food was great, and I ate every bite, but I couldn't stop thinking about dessert. The hand-frosted cakes were calling my name. I chose the red velvet cake with cream cheese icing. It was a two-layer cake, with each layer being about double the thickness of a usual cake and with a generous middle layer of icing and a healthy slathering on top. You'd better be committed if you order a slice of cake at C-Bo's: no skimpy, thin little slices of cake here.

The cake was deliciously moist, and the icing topping it off had just the right amount of sweetness without being too rich. Here's my recreation of this decadent dessert. I hope you enjoy it half as much as I did. If you get a chance to stop by C-Bo's Country Kitchen, don't forget to save room for dessert.

RED VELVET CAKE

Preheat the oven to 350 degrees. Generously grease and flour two 9-inch springform cake pans.

In a large bowl whisk together the flour, baking soda, baking powder, cocoa powder, and salt.

In another large bowl combine the sugar and vegetable oil. Whisk in the eggs, buttermilk, vanilla, and food coloring. Mix well and stir in the coffee and vinegar. Stir the flour mixture into the egg mixture.

Pour the batter evenly into the pans, and bake for 35 minutes. Do not overbake; the cake will continue to cook as it cools. Place the pans on a wire rack until the pans have cooled completely. Remove the cakes from the pan and let them stand at room temperature for two hours. Frost with your favorite cream cheese icing.

Serves 10 to 12.

2 ¼ cups all-purpose flour

1 teaspoon baking soda

1 teaspoon baking powder

3 tablespoons cocoa powder

1 teaspoon salt

2 ½ cups sugar

1 cup vegetable oil

2 large eggs

1 cup buttermilk

2 ½ teaspoons vanilla extract

2 ounces red food coloring

½ cup brewed black coffee

½ teaspoon distilled vinegar

Lasyone's Meat Pie Restaurant

Natchitoches, Louisiana

Don't let the name fool you—the founder of Lasyone's Meat Pie Restaurant in Natchitoches is anything but lazy. James Lasyone got his start as a butcher, grinding meat for Southern ladies to use in their meat pie recipes. After years of supplying the goods, James decided to make his own recipe. In 1967 he rented a space to start his "pie in the sky" dreams. Now run by his daughters, Angela and Tina, Lasyone's continues to dish out good food to its patrons.

As in most Louisiana restaurants, there's a mix of Southern and Creole traditions in this joint. If you've been paying any attention as you read through the story of my travels, you will have noticed that Southerners will deep-fry just about anything. Pies are not excluded from the madness, but in all truth, it's a smart idea to make them portable. Typically, fried pies are filled with fruit filling or even chocolate, but meat pies are also somewhat popular.

Everything on the menu at Lasyone's looked great, but my curiosity about the meat pies was piqued. The pies are usually a mix of 80 percent beef and 20 percent pork with a special blend of spices unique to the chef. The filling is placed in a piecrust that is folded over and sealed before being dropped into a deep fryer. The concept is similar to the Southwestern empanada or a "prehistoric" Hot Pocket, if you will.

I ordered the meat pie platter with dirty rice and the daily vegetable selection. When the plate arrived, I marveled at the perfect golden-brown color of the crust. Not wanting to scald myself, I gently used my fork to stab the meat pie and let the steam escape. After waiting what seemed like a reasonable amount of time, I let myself take a bite.

The crust was perfect—crispy but not overcooked—and the filling was amazing with a great mix of spices to tickle my taste buds without being too spicy. The recipe James Lasyone handed down to his daughters was definitely a winner with me. I ate every last bite and seriously considered ordering some frozen meat pies to take back home, but I was pretty certain they wouldn't make the trip well.

Here is the recipe I recreated in my own kitchen. Next time you are in Louisiana, make a trip down to Natchitoches and sample the original at Lasyone's Meat Pie Restaurant.

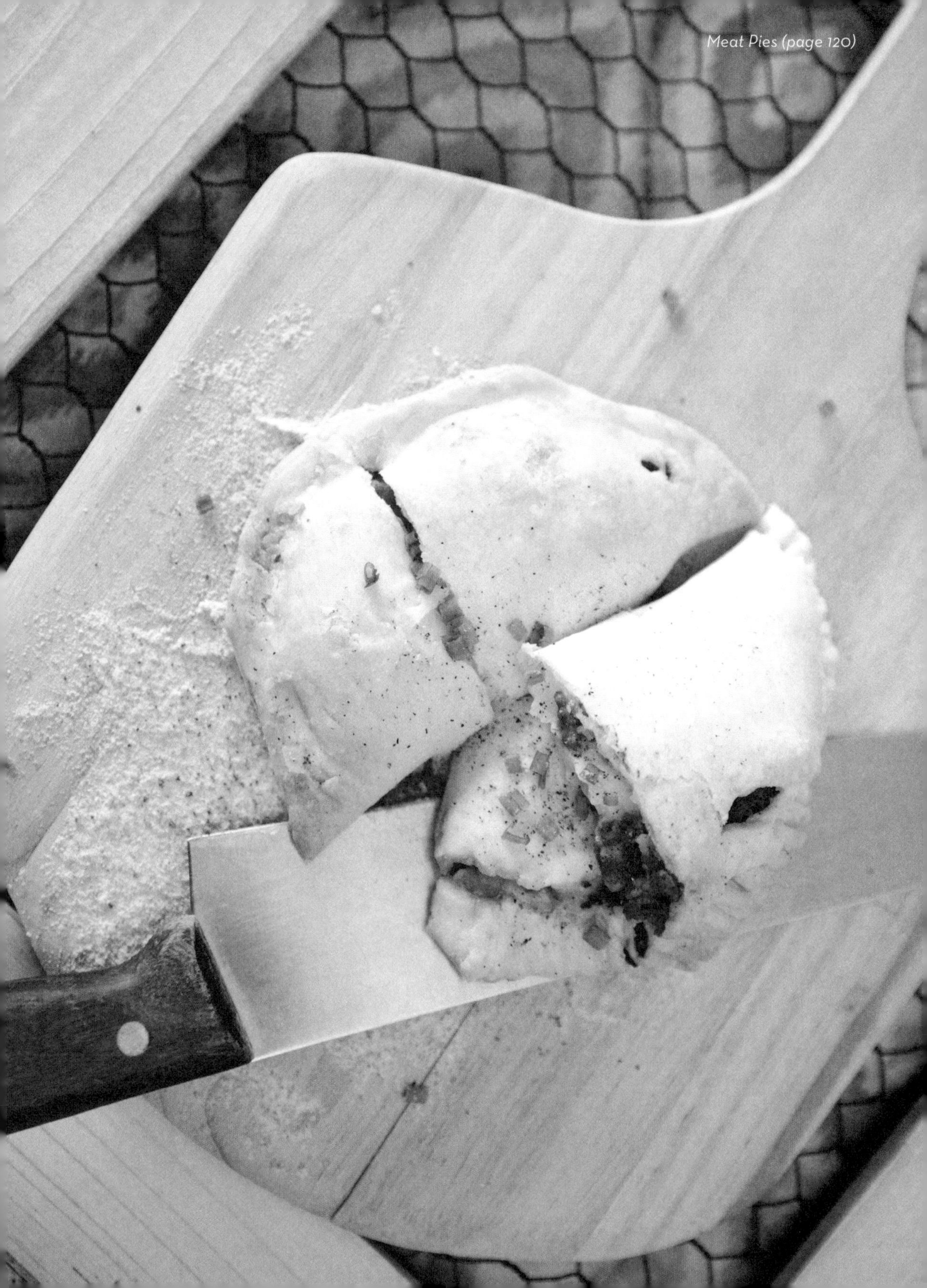

Meat Pies (page 120)

1 cup vegetable oil

½ pound ground chuck

½ pound ground pork shoulder

1 cup finely chopped onions

½ cup finely chopped celery

½ cup finely chopped green bell pepper

¼ cup finely chopped red bell pepper

2 tablespoons minced garlic

3 ½ cups beef or veal stock

Kosher salt to taste

Cracked black pepper to taste

1 tablespoon hot sauce

1 large egg, at room temperature

½ cup water

1 (15-ounce) box refrigerated piecrusts

MEAT PIES

Pour the oil into a heavy-bottomed sauté pan or cast-iron skillet and heat over medium-high heat. Add the beef and pork and cook until fully cooked and golden brown. Remove the cooked meats from the pan and reserve on a plate. Add the onions, celery, bell peppers, and garlic to the pan and cook until the vegetables are translucent but not browned. Add the meat back to the pan, reduce the heat to low, and cook for about 1 hour. Gradually add the beef stock to the pan to prevent sticking. Cook the meat pie mixture until the liquid has evaporated before removing the pan from the heat. Season liberally with salt and pepper. Add the hot sauce and fold together. Remove the pan from the heat and let the mixture cool to room temperature.

Preheat the oven to 350 degrees. Grease a large baking sheet for the pies.

Whisk the egg and water in a small bowl. Sprinkle a bit of flour on a flat surface. Place one of the piecrusts on the surface and cut 4-inch circles. Repeat until all the crusts are cut. Spoon the cooked meat mixture into the center of the circles. Brush the egg mixture around the edges of one side of the circles, fold the dough over, and press the edges with a fork to seal. Place the pies on the baking sheet. With a small knife, make small slits in the dough to vent steam. Brush the egg mixture over all the pies and bake for 20 to 25 minutes. Serve immediately.

Serves 12.

Lea's Lunchroom

Lecompte, Louisiana

There is something in my DNA that makes me love places that are steeped in history. I experienced this feeling of fondness as I listened to the tale of Lea's Lunchroom in Lecompte. In 1928 Lea Johnson opened a small, unassuming diner just off a busy state highway. He offered guests minimal choices: a plate lunch of the day, a ham sandwich, homemade pies, and strong coffee. He saw no sense in menus and stated that if the food was good, people would come back. That was eighty-six years ago, so I guess you could say that Lea was right. With the third generation of his family now running the business, Lea's Lunchroom is what I would call a success story. And Lea's personality made him famous after his appearance on the *Tonight Show* with Johnny Carson in 1989 on Thanksgiving Day, where he showed his true colors as a Louisiana gentleman.

Lea loved people, and that tradition carries on today. You can feel the warmth from his family when you walk in the doors of the classic white building with the red lettering outside. One thing that has kept this joint going is the consistency that customers experience. You can have the same delicious pie you remember from your childhood here. There still aren't any true "menus," but there has been an addition of special offerings on Sundays including fried chicken, baked turkey, baked ham, and baked chicken.

The diner has the look and feel of a place where time has stood still. I enjoyed that about it. I knew what I was coming for when I walked through the door. I wasn't there for lunch, just pie. The locals will tell you that the pies here are amazing, and I had to try them for myself. With the old-fashioned values and ambiance, I was in an all-American mood that day and decided on the apple pie.

When my slice arrived, I couldn't wait to dive in. The portion was generous, and the piecrust was a perfect golden color, flaky and sweet with a hint of salt. The fruit filling was amazing. I could tell that the pie had been hand crafted—no premade pie filling here. The apples were sweet, and the sugar and cinnamon perfectly balanced.

With such a great pie experience, I knew I had to share my joy with others. Following is my recipe for this classic pie. If you get a chance to visit Lecompte, don't hesitate to stop by Lea's Lunchroom for lunch or even just a slice of pie. You won't regret it.

APPLE PIE

1 (9-inch) piecrust

10 firm, crispy apples such as Jonagold

2 tablespoons freshly squeezed lemon juice

1 cup brown sugar

1 cup white sugar

1 cup all-purpose flour

1 teaspoon nutmeg

1 teaspoon cinnamon

1 teaspoon salt

1 cup butter

Place the piecrust in a 9-inch pie pan and bake according to recipe's instructions. Let cool.

Preheat the oven to 400 degrees.

Peel and slice the apples. Place the apples and lemon juice in a large bowl and toss together to evenly coat the apples with the juice. In another large bowl mix the brown sugar, white sugar, flour, nutmeg, cinnamon, and salt. Use the back of a fork to mix and mash out the lumps. With the same fork, cut the chilled butter into the dry mixture. Add half of the mixture to the apples and stir to coat. Pour the apple mixture into the crust and sprinkle the rest of the crumbs on top.

Cover the pie with aluminum foil and bake for 25 to 30 minutes. Remove the foil, reduce the oven temperature to 325 degrees, and continue baking, uncovered, for 20 minutes. Serve warm with your favorite ice cream.

Serves 8.

Lucille's Red Kettle Restaurant & Grill

Alexandria, Louisiana

You have to be pretty confident that what you are selling is good, quality food if you are willing to put your name on it. At that point it's not just about a brand, it's about your name. Lucille Campo, owner of Lucille's Red Kettle Restaurant and Grill in Alexandria, has just the right amount of guts and humility to pull it off. Lucille's is a simple storefront restaurant that offers simple, home-cooked breakfasts and lunches.

According to the locals, you can't find a better lunch in town. Situated next to a pawnshop, Lucille's location isn't what I would say is prime real estate, but inside the building, the atmosphere is plenty warm and inviting. The staff is friendly, and the smells coming from the kitchen make you want to take a seat and stay awhile. Lucille's isn't a fast-food stop, but if you have some time to spare on your lunch hour, it's worth every minute.

The burgers at this joint get high marks from locals and visitors alike, and the daily specials satisfy the need for a home-cooked meal. The day I happened upon Lucille's, the daily specials included beef tips, meatloaf, and shepherd's pie with a choice of three vegetables. During my travels across the South, I'd sampled my fair share of meatloaf, so the shepherd's pie sounded like a delicious alternative.

I asked the waitress for the shepherd's pie with lima beans, cabbage casserole, and corn. When my lunch arrived, I was glad I had made my choice. The mashed potato crust on the shepherd's pie was browned perfectly. It made me forget I was in a storefront restaurant and transported me, instead, to my grandmother's kitchen. The veggies were fresh and the perfect complement to this home-cooked goodness. I took one bite and felt right at home. The meat was seasoned perfectly, and the cheese paired with the potatoes so well that the sides were almost unnecessary; the pie was a complete meal in itself. I devoured it with no room left for dessert. I vowed to recreate the warm feeling I received that day. Make this at home when you need a change from the usual routine. It won't disappoint. And if you're in Alexandria and need a bite to eat after pawning that family heirloom, Lucille's Red Kettle Restaurant and Grill will fit the bill quite nicely.

SHEPHERD'S PIE

Preheat the oven to 350 degrees.

In a large skillet over medium heat, add the olive oil, onion, and carrots and cook for until softened but not browned, about 10 minutes. Increase the heat to high and add the ground chuck. Cook until it is well browned. Stir in the tomato paste and mustard, then add the stock. Whisk to combine. Add the Worcestershire sauce and salt and pepper. Reduce the heat to low and cook for 20 minutes. Pour the mixture into a 1 ½-quart casserole dish. Add the peas in an even layer and cover with the mashed potatoes. Brush the top of the mashed potatoes with the melted butter. Bake for 40 to 45 minutes, or until browned. Spoon onto plates and serve immediately.

Serves 6.

3 tablespoons olive oil

1 onion, minced

2 carrots, very finely chopped

2 pounds ground chuck

1 tablespoon tomato paste

1 teaspoon Dijon mustard

1 cup chicken stock

4 tablespoons Worcestershire sauce

Salt and pepper to taste

1 cup peas

4 cups prepared mashed potatoes

1 tablespoon butter, melted

Sharon's Café

Arcadia, Louisiana

When I pulled into the parking lot of Sharon's Café in Arcadia, I felt as though I shouldn't be driving a car, but instead hitching my horse to the post out front. The building is a small one-story structure with the old-timey awning and storefront that you might see in an old western movie. The servers don't wear uniforms, but usually jeans and a T-shirt, and it seems as though everyone in the joint knows one another. The staff is friendly and quick to help you find a seat.

There's not much to look at here, but that's probably because the focus is on feeding people good food, not getting a spread in *Better Homes & Gardens*. The prices are reasonable, and you will walk out of here very full and satisfied with an entrée, three sides, dessert, and a drink for less than ten bucks. The menu is surprisingly versatile with salads, burgers, sandwiches, and even some Mexican dishes to add a little variety. The locals guided me to the unassuming location, and boy, am I glad they did.

The dishes coming out of the kitchen looked amazing and I knew that I couldn't go wrong with whatever I chose. I finally settled on the chicken-fried steak with mashed potatoes and gravy, cabbage, and black-eyed peas. My lunch was great, and I didn't think I had room for dessert, but I had heard that they weren't to be missed. I loosened my belt and selected the lemon sheet cake.

Every morsel was worth the pain of creating the extra room in my stomach. The cake was moist and sweet with the taste of lemon in every bite, but without being too overpowering. It was like eating a cake made of lemon drops. There is something to be said for the way the cooks in the South can take a sour fruit and make it into a sweet treat you can't stop devouring. Lemon-flavored desserts are perfect for summertime, and on this hot summer day, I was glad that the folks at Sharon's Café agreed.

Here's a recreation of the lemon sheet cake I had that day. Feel free to share it with friends and family at your next summer gathering. Don't hesitate to drop by Sharon's Café in Arcadia for a taste of the real thing without breaking your bank.

LEMON SHEET CAKE

Preheat the oven to 400 degrees. Grease and flour a shallow 9 x 13-inch baking dish.

In a large bowl combine the flour, salt, baking soda, and sugar. Whisk in the sour cream and eggs until completely blended.

In a saucepan combine 1 cup of the butter, water, lemon peel, lemon juice, and 1 tablespoon of the lemon extract and bring to a full boil over medium-high heat. Remove from the heat. Stir the butter mixture into the flour mixture. Pour the batter into the baking pan.

Bake for 10 minutes, reduce the heat to 325 degrees and continue baking for 15 minutes. Let cool in the pan.

In a saucepan combine the remaining ¼ cup plus 2 tablespoons of butter, milk, and remaining 1 teaspoon of lemon extract and bring to a full boil over medium-high heat. Allow to come to 110 degrees. Quickly remove the pan from the heat. As the mixture cools, gradually add the powdered sugar, stirring until the mixture reaches a spreading consistency. Spread the icing on top of the cooled cake.

Serves 12.

2 cups all-purpose flour

1 teaspoon salt

1 teaspoon baking soda

2 cups sugar

1 cup sour cream

2 large eggs

1 ¼ cups plus 2 tablespoons butter, divided

1 cup water

2 teaspoons finely grated lemon peel

2 tablespoons lemon juice

1 tablespoon plus 1 teaspoon lemon extract, divided

¼ cup plus 2 teaspoons milk

3 ½ cups powdered sugar

The Mustard Seed

Leesville, Louisiana

The Mustard Seed in Leesville has the perfect storefront for people-watching with windows lining every square inch of the front of the building. I love people-watching almost as much as I love eating good food. That is why when locals recommended The Mustard Seed as a good place to grab a home-cooked meal, I was pleasantly surprised to find that I could combine my two loves.

The staff at The Mustard Seed put their faith on the front burner, with a Bible verse on the cover of the menu. I guess that's where the name comes into play as well. No matter what your affiliation or lack thereof, the food in this place might get you to say a hallelujah or two.

As I looked over the menu, I saw that for such a small restaurant, this place offers something for everyone—appetizers, salads, kid-friendly meals, steaks, barbecue, and ribs. Although even I enjoy a good steak every now and then, I was drawn to the veggie plate, and the number of choices was staggering. With the veggie plate, you get your choice of five veggies. I went for the mac 'n' cheese, black-eyed peas, green beans, pan-fried squash, and steamed broccoli. I threw the last one in just for those health-conscious readers out there.

When my plate arrived, I felt as though I'd hit the side item jackpot. Everything looked and smelled delicious. As I dug in, the fried squash captured my full attention. The breading was light and crispy, not overly greasy, with just the right mix of salt and pepper to complement the sweetness of the squash. I've tried to replicate it the best I can in the following recipe. But if you need a good meal when you're in Leesville, stop by The Mustard Seed and try the original for yourself. You'll be singing its praises before you leave.

PAN-FRIED SQUASH

5 yellow summer squash

1 large egg, at room temperature

1 tablespoon hot sauce

1 cup cornmeal

½ teaspoon onion powder

½ cup (1 stick) butter

Salt and pepper to taste

Cut the squash into ¼-inch thick slices. In a small bowl beat the egg and stir in the hot sauce. Pour the cornmeal and onion powder into another small bowl. Dredge each squash slice in the egg mixture and then through the cornmeal mixture. Repeat this step twice for each squash round. Place the breaded squash in a single layer on a baking sheet and refrigerate for 30 minutes.

Heat a cast-iron skillet over medium-high heat and melt a few tablespoons of butter. Fry small batches of the breaded squash until golden brown on each side, 3 to 5 minutes per side. Refrain from salting while the squash is still cooking as it will release moisture and make the squash soggy. Remove each batch of cooked squash from the pan and drain on a paper towel–lined plate. Repeat using the remaining squash and butter. Season the squash with salt and pepper while they are still hot and serve immediately.

Serves 10.

MISSISSIPPI

S ome states in the South really make an effort to display and convey the Southern way of life. Mississippi is definitely one of those states. Mississippians make it a point to tell you to slow down and not be in such a hurry, no matter what pace the rest of the world suggests. With its capital and largest city, Jackson, coming in at a population less than 300,000, it's not hard to see why Mississippi encourages maintaining a small-town feel and mindset for its visitors. It's a place that time seems to leave somewhat to itself. That's not to say that there aren't modern pieces to the puzzle of this state. I'm simply saying that instead of the times shaping Mississippi, it seems that this state maintains its ability to decide what it takes and what it leaves from the ever-changing tastes that seem to sweep across the rest of the nation.

Mississippi is made up of five very distinct regions. With rolling hills in the northeast, the delta stretching east from the Mississippi River, massive pine forests in the eastern middle section, beautiful river land in the southwest, and coastal beaches, it seems Mississippi has something for everyone. I sometimes forget that Mississippi has so much variety until I am driving the quiet roads throughout the state and the landscape slowly shifts. It's not the place to come if you are looking for fast-paced excitement, but it's the perfect place to go when you need some space and a chance to just slow life down for a minute. And in this day and age, who doesn't need that?

Cotton is king in Mississippi, and farming is a major contributor to the state's economy. With a variety of crops such as corn, peanuts, pecans, rice, sugar cane, and sweet potatoes, not to mention catfish, poultry, livestock, and dairy, this place is a meat and three owner's delight. I mean, shouldn't a state that literally "raises cane" offer some amazing sweet iced tea? It does. These people know their farmers, they know their crops, and they mean business about giving their customers a delicious home-cooked meal without the hustle and bustle of the big city.

Mississippi showed me some great hospitality and definitely left my stomach full, and in some way, my head cleared. I guess you could say the Southern charm rubbed off, helping me to slow down, loosen my belt, and enjoy all the tasty goodness the places I visited had to offer. There's soul to be found here and maybe some soul searching if you need it, and if you don't believe me, just check out the list of native-born artists—Bo Diddley, B.B. King, and Elvis, to name a few. So if you need a break from life in the big city, take a trip through Mississippi, and don't forget to slow yourself down too—none of that fast talking, fast walking, and fast driving business here. And if you forget, the locals will remind you with the utmost of sweet Southern hospitality, of course.

Bovina Café

Vicksburg, Mississippi

After much reminiscing, I have identified my favorite meal as a child, and it may surprise you. It was the Salisbury steak TV dinner, warmed in the aluminum compartment tray. I'm not sure why I have such fond memories of that mystery meat served in foil. Since my youth I've experienced much better renditions of the popular warm-and-serve dish, even as recently as my wedding. We delivered several pounds of lamb rack to the caterer and were obviously surprised to find, come dinner seating, that they chose a Salisbury steak gravy to pair with our special day's menu. It has become a standing joke in our household that at our wedding we had delicious Salisbury Lamb.

This long reminiscence of Salisbury steak brings me to a wonderful little joint named the Bovina Café, smack in the middle of Vicksburg, the seat of Warren County. The town is one of my new favorite destinations for outstanding Southern food and has quite the collection of remarkable meat and three joints. At Bovina Café the exterior of the building is nothing all that special; however, the sign gets straight to the point: "Good Home Cooking." I was confident in my choice, but I couldn't take all the credit for choosing the Bovina Café since every local I met recommended this little spot more than once.

Inside the restaurant, it was fun and no fuss. The mostly yellow and red walls boasted some of the local taxidermist's finest work the way paintings would, perhaps, in a different establishment. I was immediately overwhelmed with absolutely delicious smells emanating from the kitchen—wonderful, sweet, yeasty goodness from baking rolls and sweet caramel from the onions simmering on the stove. What I ordered was by far the best choice I could have made on that sticky, dreary day in Vicksburg.

Remember my youthful memories of the Salisbury steak? Well, there was a point to that rambling. I went directly for a home run—the hamburger steak on the daily special menu. The rest of my plate was mashed potatoes, cornbread, very meaty and delicious green beans, and field peas. But in the center of the plate was a mounded burger patty that smelled, looked, and tasted like my most favorite childhood entrée, Salisbury steak. The aromatics, seasoning, and texture of the dish proved that someone with skill had prepared the eight ounces of juicy, tender ground meat, covered in onions and a little dollop of the pan juice. As I neared the end of my hamburger steak, I felt as though I was losing something special. I enjoyed my meal, experience and reliving my youth at the Bovina Café, and wish I could do it again and again. It's those fond memories—likely created by a significant life event, but recalled by a food ingredient, smell, or taste—that leave me at a loss for words. The weather wasn't cooperating, the building may have been misleading, and the enormous deer heads peppering the walls may have thrown me for a loop, but I ended up with a wonderful way to spend the afternoon in Vicksburg, enjoying the hamburger steak and revisiting my childhood.

Hamburger Steak (page 136)

1 pound 80 percent lean ground beef

1 tablespoon Worcestershire sauce

1 teaspoon Montreal steak seasoning

Salt and pepper to taste

1 teaspoon chopped fresh garlic

1 teaspoon canola oil

1 large Vidalia onion, sliced

1 cup beef stock

4 tablespoons all-purpose flour

1 tablespoon butter

HAMBURGER STEAK

In a large bowl mix the ground beef with the Worcestershire sauce, steak seasoning, salt, pepper, and garlic. Gently fold the ingredients together, using your hand or a spoon, until completely incorporated.

Heat a large skillet over medium heat. Divide the meat mixture in half and pat out two patties, about 2 inches thick. Add the oil to the pan. When the oil is barely smoking, add the patties to the pan. Cook until browned on one side, about 4 minutes. Flip the patties and add the onions to the pan. Reduce the heat to medium-low. Cook until the onions are lightly browned and translucent, about 10 minutes. Increase the heat to medium-high and add the beef stock. Bring the stock to a full boil and allow to reduce, 3 to 5 minutes. Remove the patties and reserve on a plate for serving.

Add the flour and butter to the stock mixture, whisking constantly until the flour begins to thicken the gravy. Taste and add more salt and pepper if needed.

Cover the hamburger steaks with the onion and gravy mixture and serve immediately.

Serves 2.

Café Anchuca

Vicksburg, Mississippi

Just when you think you have enjoyed every variation, style, and flavor note that could possibly be offered by a Southern meat and three, you are immediately knocked out of your rocking chair with a restaurant that is the epitome of the real Southern food experience. The place I'm referring to is Café Anchuca in Vicksburg, and it's changed my thoughts about chocolate bourbon pecan pie forever.

Would you like to start with the Georgia Comeback Shrimp, the Anchuca Seafood Gumbo, or the Comeback Salad? "Don't mind if I do. Let me try them all." These were my exact words, and thank God for the server at Café Anchuca. She was very aware of my hunger pains and knew exactly what side of the menu to offer me first. Service at the café is without flaw, the food is simple and tasty, and the atmosphere is preserved in time. Anchuca is a Choctaw Indian word that means "happy home." It's a fitting name for this wonderful location. I think the name should also mean "happy tummy." The property is unlike any other Southern restaurant I've visited on this journey. Local politician and coal and ice merchant J.W. Mauldin built the original house in 1830. During the Civil War the home provided shelter to those severely wounded in battle. Today the home is listed on the National Register of Historic Places. The expansive grounds and buildings offer guests B&B-style accommodations.

Typical meat and three restaurants in the South are family-operated and offer a consistent vibe that says "sit down, relax, this isn't fast-food, and hush until your food is served." These are all the qualities I look for when seeking my favorite Southern joints.

Beyond my three-part first course and the gallon of sweet tea, I noted classically prepared Southern dishes on the menu, but there were also notes of creativity and regional items that were unfamiliar to me. My dinner was amazing. I felt transformed to another time and place—as if the history and artifacts surrounding me were seeping into my meal. The ambiance was happy and relaxed, not formal, but polished, reminding me of a lunch or dinner at the home of a distant relative whose ability to decorate and cook I covet.

History and food is almost as important as history and family. Traditions are built and maintained by our connections through food. They help us grow, while reminding us always not to stray too far. The vivid memories I have of learning to knead biscuits with my grandmother are responsible for my love affair with cooking, food history, and ingredients. As I raise my own children, I'm reminded of my memories and nudged to share them. The overwhelming workday, deadlines, and obligations in life distance us from our memories. How many more generations will have a "kneading a biscuit" memory? With convenience food and busy schedules, the dangerous balancing act is lopsided. It's easy for me to pop a can of biscuits, and however unlikely it may seem, it's possible they may be tasty. But the true meaning of this journey is to preserve those biscuit memories. Slow down and savor the biscuits, share the recipe, and pass on the memories. This is something that Café Anchuca is doing perfectly.

I slowed down and enjoyed my meal, and to close the experience I finished with pie, although I think calling it pie won't do it justice. Café Anchuca served me the best chocolate bourbon pecan pie I've ever tasted. The buttery, flaky crust held crunchy local pecans and a bourbon-infused chocolate custard that should be bottled and sold as you leave the building. I prayed for a miracle that they would share the recipe. The pie has been served since the café first opened its doors, and the recipe is half-written, half-memorized, and all secret. On my drive out of Vicksburg that evening, I realized how lucky I was to stumble upon such a wonderful food find. That pie is a memory that I can share with you—along with my recreation of the recipe. Make it at home with your children or friends. Use it as a starting point in the kitchen to create memories that will last forever.

Chocolate Bourbon Pecan Pie (page 140)

1 ¼ cups all-purpose flour

1 tablespoon sugar

¼ teaspoon salt

¾ cup cold butter, cubed

½ cup buttermilk, chilled

1 ¼ cups sugar

1 cup dark corn syrup

3 large eggs

¼ teaspoon salt

1 teaspoon vanilla extract

¼ cup butter, melted

4 tablespoons bourbon

1 cup chopped pecans

5 ounces chocolate pieces, chopped

CHOCOLATE BOURBON PECAN PIE

For the crust, in a large bowl sift the flour, sugar, and salt. Add the butter and use your fingers to work it into the flour mixture. Create a well in the center of the mixture and pour in the chilled buttermilk. Use a fork to stir the dough together.

Lightly flour a work surface. Dump out the dough mixture and gently knead into a ball. Wrap the ball in plastic wrap and refrigerate for at least 2 hours.

Roll out the piecrust on a well-floured surface to about ⅛ inch thick and 12 to 14 inches in diameter. Place the dough in a pie pan, letting the dough hang over the rim. Fold the edges under and crimp with your fingers. Cover with plastic wrap and refrigerate while you make the filling.

For the filling, in a large bowl mix together the sugar, corn syrup, eggs, salt, vanilla, butter, and bourbon. Whisk until completely incorporated and free of lumps.

Preheat the oven to 350 degrees.

Pour the pecans and chopped chocolate into the bottom of the piecrust. Pour the filling over the chocolate and nuts.

Place the pie on a baking sheet and bake on the center rack for 35 to 45 minutes. To test if the pie is completely cooked, jiggle the baking sheet. If the center has only a slight wiggle, remove the pie from the oven and let it stand on the counter for 20 minutes. The filling will continue to cook as it stands.

Serves 8.

Café on Main

Columbus, Mississippi

The magical smell of baking bread hypnotizes the senses. With bread ready to grab and bake at any local grocery store these days, the smell of homemade fresh-baked bread is somewhat of a rarity, but well worth seeking out. The great thing about most meat and three restaurants is that they are not at all about "convenience" food. And they expect customers to understand that what they are putting in their mouths is "home cooking" and not to be rushed. From my tasting adventure, I've learned some things are definitely worth waiting for and that some of the tastiest treats are the small things that are often overlooked.

This brings me to the Café on Main in Columbus. Originally housed in the basement of an old building, this downtown restaurant is now on the ground floor of a former department store. If you ask anyone in town, they will tell you that Café on Main has some of the best sweet tea and cakes you could ask for in a Southern town. Frequently chosen for the best plate lunch by the locals, Café on Main has the bases covered when it comes to delicious Southern fare.

As I sat down to eat, I was greeted with the traditional setup of a meat and three restaurant: entrées with the choice of veggies and sides. There were no wrong turns to take at this joint, from what I had heard, and when my order arrived, I was not disappointed. From the fried catfish with the hushpuppies, to the earthy black-eyed peas and melt-in-my-mouth turnip greens, the meal left me stuffed and satisfied.

But it was the often overlooked and underappreciated accompaniment at Café on Main that stole the show for me. With my plate, I was given the choice of cornbread or a roll. After smelling the lovely warm, sweet yeasty smell of freshly baked rolls coming from the kitchen, I don't even think I had a choice at that point. The aroma of the freshly baked bread summoned me, and I came like a little puppy. When my lunch was delivered, I tore into the delicious roll, and one bite made me feel as though I was back in my grandma's kitchen.

I put on my best Southern manners when I asked for the recipe, but I should have known that a joint famous for its baked goods would not be keen on sharing its recipes. So I have put together my own, and even if it's not the original, it will still give you the warm fuzzies when you make it at home and the house fills with the delicious smell of warm bread. Don't be surprised if the kids actually race to the table for this one. And if you've never experienced it, or just need a memory refresher, head down to Café on Main in Columbus, and let your nostrils do the walking.

YEAST ROLLS

1 (.25-ounce) package active dry yeast

1 cup warm water, 105 to 115 degrees

2 tablespoons sugar

2 tablespoons vegetable oil

½ teaspoon kosher salt

1 large egg

2 ½ cups all-purpose flour, divided

Softened butter for greasing the baking pan

Melted butter for brushing on rolls

Combine the yeast and water in a glass bowl. Whisk in the sugar. Cover and let stand until the yeast begins to bubble, about 15 minutes. Add the oil, salt, and egg to the yeast mixture and stir well. Add 1 cup of the flour, stirring until smooth, creamy, and frothy. Cover the bowl with a cloth and let rise 15 minutes.

Grease a 9-inch square baking pan with softened butter.

Scrape down the sides of the bowl and add remaining 1 ½ cups flour. Stir until mixed. Turn the dough out onto a lightly floured work surface, and knead for 3 minutes.

Using about 2 tablespoons of dough for each roll, shape into about 16 balls. Arrange in pan. Cover and let rise until doubled, 15 to 20 minutes.

Preheat oven to 425 degrees.

Bake the rolls for 12 to 15 minutes. Remove from oven and brush them with melted butter.

Serves 16.

Clancy's Café

Red Banks, Mississippi

I don't know if there is a rulebook for owners of Southern meat and three restaurants that guides them in food preparation, side choices, and decor, but after visiting so many on my journey I am somewhat convinced that there has to be, even if it is unwritten. When you walk into the dining room of Clancy's Café in Red Banks, you feel the familiar warmth of wood paneling on the walls, and you know you are at home here.

Owner and chef Tyler Clancy opened the joint in 2011 to feed the hungry masses of Red Banks. With a degree in hospitality management and kitchen experience at two famous restaurants in Oxford, Mississippi—City Grocery and Emileigh's Table—Tyler knows Southern cooking and how to make customers happy. That's what keeps people coming back to Clancy's Café.

The menu tells you everything you need to know about Clancy's in big, bold letters—"Southern soul and smoke." I knew exactly what flavors were headed my way, and I could hardly wait. Clancy's is known for catfish and barbecue, but I decided to travel off the beaten path. I chose the butterflied chicken breast stuffed with spinach and artichoke dip, the pickled green tomatoes, and green beans. Clancy's does a great job of taking traditional Southern dishes and tweaking them to a new level.

As I devoured every bite of the scrumptious plate, I was pleasantly surprised by the pickled green tomatoes. I am a fan of pickled anything, to be honest, and having lived in the South for some time now, I have also become a huge fan of green tomatoes. They are slightly tart, and they lend themselves well to being pickled. Clancy's did a great job of capturing the natural tartness of the green tomatoes while keeping them from getting too soft or slimy. I imagined pairing them with all kinds of entrées and even throwing them on a sandwich at home.

The following recipe captures the essence of Clancy's delicious pickled green. Serve them with anything that catches your fancy or just enjoy them on their own. And if you happen to pass through Red Banks, be sure to stop by Clancy's Café for some delicious food and the original recipe.

2 pounds green tomatoes

4 cloves garlic

4 sprigs fresh dill

4 sprigs fresh rosemary

2 cups cider vinegar

2 cups water

2 tablespoons salt

2 tablespoons sugar

1 tablespoon whole black peppercorns

½ teaspoon crushed red pepper flakes

PICKLED GREEN TOMATOES

Slice the tomatoes into ¼-inch thick slices. Divide tomatoes, garlic, dill, and rosemary among 4 clean glass pint jars, packing the tomatoes tightly in each jar.

In a saucepan combine vinegar, water, salt, sugar, peppercorns, and red pepper flakes. Bring to a boil and cook over medium-high heat until the sugar is completely dissolved.

Pour the warm brine over the pickles, filling the jars to within ¼ inch of the top. Make sure all of the tomatoes are fully submerged. Screw on the jar lids and refrigerate for 7 to 10 days before opening and serving.

Makes 4 pints.

Doretha's Restaurant & Lounge

Summit, Mississippi

While traveling throughout the South to find the tastiest meat and three restaurants, I have visited tons of places with loads of character, but none quite compare to Doretha's Restaurant and Lounge in Summit. Where else can you enjoy a family-friendly atmosphere while eating a shrimp po' boy with the kids, only to return later to what has transformed into a nightclub? Talk about a split personality!

The people in Summit have nothing but great things to say about the food and service at Doretha's, so I headed over to check it out. The staff at Doretha's was extremely friendly and welcoming, the atmosphere was warm and inviting, and I settled in to peruse the menu.

I was tempted by many of the options laid before me. Plenty of the locals had raved about the burgers, but I knew that if I was going to continue my long journey, I needed something more substantial than a burger to get me through the lonesome miles that lay ahead. And then I spotted the perfect and simple sustaining choice—the red beans and rice.

Red beans and rice began in the southeast as a Monday night meal. It was a way to make use of the leftover ham from Sunday dinner in a dish that simmered along throughout the day, needing little tending. The beans could cook while the woman of the household tackled the week's laundry. Over the years, it has become a staple of the Southeast.

As my server placed my dish before me, I could smell the delicious Cajun seasonings, onions, and peppers in the steaming bowl. With my vinegar-based hot sauce by my side, I was ready to take a trip to flavor town. I enjoyed every last spoonful and was reminded, yet again, of how the simplest dishes often bring me the most pleasure.

The recipe I've included may be simple, but it's always a crowd pleaser and is guaranteed to leave everyone feeling satisfied. If you are in Summit, stop by Doretha's for their version, and who knows? Maybe the spices will inspire you to stick around a little later for a dance or two.

RED BEANS AND RICE

Place the beans in a large pot and cover with 4 inches of water. Add a pinch of salt. Bring to a boil over medium-high heat and cook, uncovered, for 10 minutes. Reduce the heat to low and simmer for 30 minutes. Cover the pot, remove from the heat, and let stand for 1 hour.

In a large cast-iron skillet, cook the bacon over medium heat until crisp. Add the onions, bell peppers, and celery to the pan and cook until they begin to caramelize, about 15 minutes. Add the garlic, black pepper, cayenne, basil, oregano, and bay leaves.

Pour the beans into a colander to drain. Add the beans to the bacon mixture. Continue cooking over medium heat.

Slice the sausage into ¼-inch chunks. In a separate skillet, heat the oil until shimmering, add the sausage, and cook over medium heat until browned, 8 to 10 minutes. Add the sausage to the bean mixture.

Add the water to the bean mixture and bring to a simmer over medium-high heat. Reduce the heat to medium-low and cook, uncovered, for 2 hours. When the beans are done, serve the chunky ragout over the cooked rice with plenty of the potlikker.

Serves 8.

1 pound dried red kidney beans

Pinch of kosher salt, plus more to taste

1 pound applewood smoked bacon, finely chopped

1 large onion, finely chopped

1 green bell pepper, finely chopped

1 rib celery, finely chopped

2 cloves garlic, minced

Freshly cracked black pepper to taste

¼ teaspoon cayenne pepper

1 teaspoon dried basil

1 teaspoon dried oregano

2 bay leaves

12 ounces andouille sausage, sliced

2 tablespoons vegetable oil

2 quarts water

6 cups cooked white rice

Mama Jo's Country Cookin' Restaurant

Oxford, Mississippi

If you've ever heard the saying, "If mama ain't happy, ain't nobody happy," then you will be a welcome customer at Mama Jo's Country Cookin' Restaurant in Oxford. Don't get me wrong, Joester Egerson Brassell, known as Mama Jo, is a sweet little lady who just wants to fill your belly with good home cooking. But one glance around at the signs in the restaurant, and you will see that you had better have your attitude straight before you walk in the doors. Above the register are several signs that let customers know there will be an "upcharge" for dealing with customers with bad attitudes.

That being said, Mama Jo is a delightful Southern lady who truly values family. The many pictures of her family and friends make you feel as though you've walked into someone's living room and are meeting the kinfolk. She makes sure to let her customers know that nothing here comes from a can, and everything is made with lots of love and passion. According to Mama Jo, love is the main ingredient in any recipe. "If you ain't got no love in your cooking, you ain't got no good cooking. You have got to have the love," she says.

The food here is heaven sent. Mama Jo says that her talent in cooking is her spiritual gift. She wakes up at night thinking of the recipes sent from the Man Upstairs and writes them down to use in her restaurant. Just as I said—heaven sent—and one bite of Mama Jo's cooking will instill faith in you.

The dining room is small and plainly decorated, and the staff, complete with hairnets, serve customers cafeteria-style from a counter covered in the traditional plexiglass. Each customer gets a plate loaded with an entrée and a few sides, complete with cornbread or a roll. My plate was heavy as I carried it back to my table, and I almost dropped my cornbread. Man, am I glad that I didn't, though. Everything was good, but Mama Jo nailed the cornbread. It was sweet and moist with a buttery goodness that made me feel warm inside.

I can't say that I got my recipe for cornbread through a spiritual revelation, but I hope its great taste will lift your spirits for a moment or two. And if you're looking for a delicious meal with one of the nicest ladies you could hope to meet, stop by Mama Jo's when you pass through Oxford, but don't forget to bring your manners.

CORNBREAD

Grease an 8-inch cast-iron skillet with the vegetable shortening. Place the pan in the oven and preheat to 400 degrees.

Combine the cornmeal, flour, baking powder, sugar, and salt in a large bowl. In a separate bowl whisk the milk, eggs, and melted butter. Pour the milk mixture into the cornmeal mixture and whisk until well incorporated.

Remove the pan from the oven and lightly grease with more vegetable oil or lard. Pour the batter into the pan and return it to the oven. Bake the cornbread for 25 to 30 minutes, until a wooden pick inserted near the center comes out clean. Let stand for 10 to 15 minutes before cutting onto wedges.

Serves 6 to 8.

2 tablespoons vegetable shortening or lard for greasing

1 ½ cups cornmeal

1 ½ cups all-purpose flour

4 tablespoons baking powder

3 tablespoons sugar

1 ½ teaspoons salt

1 ½ cups milk

2 large eggs

2 tablespoons melted butter

Mammy's Cupboard

Natchez, Mississippi

There is an incredible story behind the absolutely strange building called Mammy's Cupboard in Natchez. The building is in the form of a giant 200-foot Aunt Jemima-type figure with windows and a door cut into the bell-shaped red skirt. It used to be a gas station and was built by Henry Gaude between 1939 and 1940 during the *Gone with the Wind* craze to attract visitors from the highway. It worked, and Mammy's became a roadhouse diner, but by the 1990s, she needed some love. The building was in desperate need of a paint job, and Mammy's arms were broken off.

In 1994 Doris Kemp came along to revitalize the old girl, introducing a new menu and repairing and repainting the structure itself, with the color of the figure's skin getting a little lighter in the process. Mammy's has been a topic of controversy for a while, but no one argues about the food. Lorna Martin, the current owner, has stayed true to Doris's original menu, and it seems to keep the guests coming back. Everything is made from scratch, and there are specials offered daily. Lorna's mother, Mary, can often be found running the cash register.

The cakes, pies, and breads at Mammy's are baked fresh daily and provide a very welcoming scent to walk into. The dining room is small but quaint and well decorated. It's a bit hard to forget, though, that you're having lunch under a giant woman's skirt.

As I looked over the menu, I was drawn to the sandwich section. They didn't sound fancy, but often, it's the no-frills dishes that blow me away. And the delicious scents I enjoyed while walking in may have been guiding me as well. After a few minutes, I decide on Mammy's Chicken Salad Sandwich—pulled chicken breast mixed with bits of pineapple and almonds flavored with ginger and curry, served on top of sourdough bread. It wasn't a typical Southern chicken salad but absolutely delicious nonetheless. The bread was thick, white, and fluffy and served as a perfect pillow-like base for the generous portion of creamy chicken salad with just the right amount of crunch from the almonds and sweetness from the pineapple. The potato salad and coleslaw that come on the plate were also very yummy, but the chicken salad was definitely the star.

No matter what you think about the building itself and what it may or may not represent in the history of this country, the food at Mammy's Cupboard is fantastic. Lorna wouldn't share her chicken salad recipe, but I've included one. Enjoy it as a picnic lunch on a nice summer day. When you pass through Natchez, don't forget to stop by Mammy's Cupboard to take in the sights, the tastes, and the smells.

CHICKEN SALAD

3 pounds boneless, skinless chicken breasts

1 tablespoon plus 1 teaspoon salt, divided

5 large hard-boiled eggs

5 ribs celery, finely chopped (about 2 ½ cups)

2 cups minced sweet pickles

1 ¼ cups mayonnaise

¾ teaspoon white pepper

Place the chicken in a saucepan and cover with 3 inches of water. Season with 1 tablespoon of salt and bring to a boil over medium-high heat. Reduce the heat to low and simmer until chicken is thoroughly cooked and tender, 15 to 20 minutes. Remove the chicken from the pan and set aside to cool.

Peel the eggs and grate them into a large bowl. Shred the chicken with a fork and cut across the shreds to create smaller pieces. Add the chicken to the eggs. Add the celery, pickles, mayonnaise, remaining 1 teaspoon salt, and pepper. Stir until the chicken is coated with mayonnaise. Serve immediately or refrigerate until thoroughly cooled.

Serves 12.

Martha's Menu

Corinth, Mississippi

Corinth is small-town America through and through, and Martha's Menu is the perfect place to get back to the basics. The building sits on the square of the historic downtown and isn't anything special from the outside—plain yellowish brick and a faded hand-painted sign with the name of the joint and the phone number. But as your momma always said, it's not what's on the outside that counts, it's what's on the inside, right?

I'm not talking about the decor, though. I'm talking about the tasty treats and savory smells that you will find when you walk through the door. If you are expecting super-speedy service and a generic smile, you may be in the wrong place. That is not a judgment, just an observation. Things move slower here, and this isn't exactly the place to rake in the high-dollar tips. The owners have kept the prices low over the years, which is great for customers, but maybe not so great for the waitstaff. That being said, the staff is friendly and moves at the speed of the rest of the state.

As I looked over the menu and the daily specials, I noticed some variations on classic dishes, such as ham and dumplings, and some traditional Southern favorites, such as pig brains and eggs. I am sure to the unseasoned Southern traveler, some of these dishes may sound like a circus sideshow, but if I've learned anything from being a chef, it's that you have to try it before you say you don't like it. Just ask Andrew Zimmern, host of *Bizarre Foods* on the Travel Channel. Some of the strangest parts of the animal are the most delicious.

I think that Andrew would approve of my lunch selection at Martha's Menu: fried chicken livers. They were coated in a crispy batter with just the right amount of salt and pepper and cooked perfectly, preserving the creamy texture and earthy flavor of the livers themselves. My sides of creamed potatoes, green beans, and cornbread were also amazing, but I was happy to have made my chicken-livered choice (pun intended).

Chicken livers are inexpensive, easy to find, and very simple to prepare. Just follow this recipe to experience the richness of this tasty dish. And the next time you're in Corinth and not in too much of a hurry, pop by Martha's Menu for a hot lunch and a great value.

FRIED CHICKEN LIVERS

1 pound fresh chicken livers

2 cups buttermilk

1 cup all-purpose flour

1 tablespoon kosher salt, plus more for sprinkling

½ tablespoon freshly cracked black pepper, plus more for sprinkling

4 cups vegetable oil

Pinch of cayenne pepper

Drain the livers and rinse thoroughly. Place them in a bowl and pour in the buttermilk. Let the livers soak for 1 hour. Combine the flour, salt, and pepper in a medium bowl or shallow baking dish.

Remove the livers from the buttermilk and place them on a plate. Lightly sprinkle the livers with salt and pepper. Dredge the livers in the seasoned flour.

Pour the oil into a deep skillet. Heat over high heat until shimmering. Carefully place the livers in the hot oil and fry until golden brown, 2 to 3 minutes. Flip once to cook other side.

When the livers are golden brown, remove them from the oil and place on a paper towel–lined plate to drain. Check the seasoning and add more salt and pepper if needed while the crunchy breading is still hot. Sprinkle with cayenne.

Serves 4.

The Cottage Tea Room

Coffeeville, Mississippi

Established in 2011, the Cottage Tea Room in Coffeeville may not have the years of service that some of the other joints I've visited along my journey have, but it still has a strong sense of family and tradition.

When I hear the words "tea room," I picture a group of silver-haired ladies wearing white gloves while sitting around a doily-lined table and sipping tea from fine china with their pinkies stuck out. I think of tiny, dainty, unappealing tea sandwiches made of cucumbers or the thinnest slathering of tuna or pimento cheese. But the Cottage Tea Room has none of those things. The food here is anything but dainty, and although there may be some silver-haired ladies in the mix, they are hardly the white-glove crowd. Instead, the plates coming out of the kitchen are filled to the edges with hearty helpings of home cooking. The burgers will convince you that the restaurant name is perhaps a misnomer. The shrimp and grits plate makes the waitresses arms quiver from the sheer weight. You won't leave hungry, that's for sure.

After looking at all the delicious dishes coming out of the kitchen, I knew I had a tough choice to make. I looked over the menu and settled on the poppy seed chicken with squash casserole and butter beans. Every bite was delicious, but the squash casserole won the blue ribbon for being my favorite here.

The squash was perfectly seasoned, with a touch of sweetness that was complemented by the onions. The creamy mixture of butter, mayonnaise, and cheese turns this light vegetable into a decadent side. The crispy bread and cracker crumb topping with melted butter was just the right finish for this tasty side. I inhaled the casserole, no raised pinky in sight, and marveled at the wonders of this Southern creation.

I was excited to get back to my kitchen and master the recipe for myself. And now I'm sharing it with you, just as the Cottage Tea Room in Coffeeville shared its wonders with me. Make sure that you bring your family together to enjoy this tasty yellow goodness.

SQUASH CASSEROLE

Preheat the oven to 350 degrees. Grease a 9-inch casserole dish with cooking spray.

Melt 2 tablespoons of the butter in a sauté pan. Add the onions and cook, stirring occasionally, until translucent, about 10 minutes. Add the squash and cook, stirring occasionally, until tender, 10 to 15 minutes. Remove from the heat and let cool slightly.

Place the eggs in a large bowl and whisk well. Add the cheese and milk and whisk until all the ingredients are well incorporated. Add the squash and onions and stir to combine.

In the same pan melt the remaining 2 tablespoons butter. Add the cayenne, salt, and pepper. Stir well to combine. Place the cracker crumbs in a bowl. Pour the butter mixture over the crackers and stir until the crumbs are thoroughly moistened.

Pour the squash mixture into the baking dish. Top evenly with buttered cracker crumbs. Place in the oven and bake, uncovered, for 15 minutes. Increase the oven temperature to 400 degrees and cook the squash for another 15 minutes, or until the top is browned. Let stand 10 minutes before serving.

Serves 8.

4 tablespoons butter, divided

1 yellow onion, finely chopped

6 cups 1/4-inch sliced yellow squash

2 large eggs

1 cup grated Cheddar cheese

1 cup milk

1/4 teaspoon cayenne pepper

1/2 teaspoon kosher salt

1/2 teaspoon freshly cracked black pepper

1 sleeve buttery crackers (such as Ritz), crushed

The Farmstead Restaurant

Columbus, Mississippi

Columbus prides itself on being a friendly place, and when you walk into the Farmstead Restaurant, you'll think that the staff received the town memo. As the home of the Mississippi University for Women, Columbus is somewhat of a college town, but the people who live here year-round make sure that whether you're here for the fall semester, just passing through, or setting down roots, you are made to feel welcome. On the restaurant's Facebook page, the staff promises "all the Southern hospitality you can handle," and from my experience, that's not an empty promise.

Inside the restaurant, I was greeted with smiling faces and a large, open dining room with wood-paneled walls covered with antique pictures and a big green chalkboard on the wall listing the daily specials. For a minute, I had a sinking feeling that I was going to have to miss recess and beat out the erasers again. But the friendly staff pulled me back from my flashback and invited me to pull up a chair.

To start my meal, the waiter placed some fried okra, hot sauce, and a glass of ice water on my table. What else could a man ask for? I was already happy I made the trip to this little joint. As I looked over the menu, my eyes kept wandering back to the green chalkboard to look over the daily specials. There was a choice of fried chicken, hamburger steak, hash brown casserole, or grilled chicken breast. The list

of sides was even more impressive, including speckled butter beans, creamed potatoes and gravy, creamed corn, turnip greens, green beans, and sweet potato casserole—and that's not the full list! It seemed to be quite the undertaking for the kitchen to attempt such an array, but none of the staff seemed weary, so I took that as a good sign. I decided on the grilled chicken breast with speckled butter beans, green beans, and sweet potato casserole. I was somewhat weary from all the fried food I'd been eating lately, and the grilled chicken seemed to be the perfect break. I wasn't disappointed with my choice, but the true winner on my plate was the sweet potato casserole.

The potatoes were creamy and whipped to perfection with just the right amount of butter, brown sugar, and a touch of nutmeg to have me scooping up every last bite. Despite my lighter choice, the sweet potato casserole was so sweet and decadent that I thought I had ordered dessert for dinner.

Sweet potatoes are a great choice when it comes to getting kids to eat their vegetables. They're a fun color and sweet all by themselves. Use the following recipe to get your young'uns to the table—you won't have a fight on your hands. And anytime you're passing through Columbus, be sure to stop by the Farmstead Restaurant for a hearty helping of sweet potato casserole and Southern hospitality.

SWEET POTATO CASSEROLE

For the sweet potatoes, preheat the oven to 400 degrees.

Using a small knife, pierce the sweet potatoes several times and place on a baking sheet. Bake about 45 minutes, until tender. Let cool slightly. Slice the potatoes into halves lengthwise. Scoop out the pulp and place it in a large bowl. Using a potato masher or a fork, mash the pulp until smooth.

Reduce the oven temperature to 375 degrees. Butter a 2-quart baking dish with 1 tablespoon butter.

Place the eggs in a large bowl. Whisk well. Add the white sugar and remaining 3/4 cup butter and stir well. Add the milk and vanilla and stir well. Spoon in 3 1/2 cups of the mashed sweet potatoes a little at a time and stir until well incorporated. Spoon the mixture into the baking pan.

For the topping, mix together the brown sugar, flour, butter, and pecans. Stir until crumbly. Sprinkle the topping over the sweet potatoes. Bake for 30 minutes, or until the top is browned and the sweet potatoes are thoroughly heated.

Serves 10.

Sweet Potatoes

3 medium sweet potatoes (about 1 pound)

3/4 cup plus 1 tablespoon butter, softened

3 large eggs, at room temperature

1 1/4 cups white sugar

1/2 cup milk, at room temperature

1 teaspoon vanilla extract

Candied Pecan Topping

1/2 cup packed brown sugar

1/3 cup all-purpose flour

2 tablespoons butter, softened

3/4 cup chopped toasted pecans

The Senator's Place

Cleveland, Mississippi

Often around the dinner table, you'll hear a mix of topics being discussed, including food and politics. At the Senator's Place in Cleveland, you may be even more likely to hear these topics come up. The owner, Willie L. Simmons, has been in the Mississippi state senate since 1993. He has owned the restaurant since 2003, moving it from its original location to its current location in 2005. But don't worry, politics is not the meat and potatoes of this joint—the meat and potatoes are.

Willie is as down to earth as you can get. He's not decked out in a politician's suit and tie when he's on the job here, just a simple T-shirt, ball cap, and blue apron. He may be shaking hands and kissing babies, but he's in the dining room, not on the campaign trail.

The Senator's Place is a plain brick building with a sign outside that reads, "Delicious food for the soul." Inside the restaurant, a single-line buffet bar holds the plates and the hot food. Offerings change daily but usually consist of a choice of four entrées and five or six sides with hot cornbread and rolls and dessert. The place is usually open only for lunch, but if you're in town on a Friday night, you can enjoy dinner as well. The dining room is open with several small, square tables peppered throughout and minimal decorations adorning the plain white walls. The focus here is on the food.

As I walked in, I was again bucked off of my anti-buffet high horse. A friendly waitress took my drink order, but from there, the service was up to me. On the buffet were fried chicken, smoked chicken, neck bones, and smothered chicken—it was a good thing I was in the mood for chicken. I chose the smoked chicken because the smell alone made my mouth water. Candied yams, Cajun red beans, and cabbage rounded out my order. As I carried what seemed like four pounds of food back to my table, I knew I was in for a treat.

Every bite was amazing, but the smoked chicken made me want to elect Willie to the White House. Anyone who can cook a chicken like that, so moist and flavorful, can surely run the country. I begged Willie for his secrets, but as we all know, politicians have tight lips, so I was forced to recreate the smoked chicken in the following recipe. The next time you're feeling as though there's nothing good about politics, stop by The Senator's Place in Cleveland for a smoked chicken pick-me-up.

SMOKED CHICKEN

Place the salt, sugar, basil, peppercorns, chives, and lemon in a large pot. Add the water. Bring to a boil over medium-high heat. Reduce the heat to low and simmer for 10 minutes. Remove from the heat and let cool to room temperature. Rinse chicken and place in the brine. Refrigerate for 12 hours or overnight.

Remove chicken from brine and pat dry. Sprinkle additional salt and pepper on the chicken. Using kitchen twine, tie the legs together and the wings tightly against the body if desired.

Prepare the smoker for cooking. Allow the temperature to reach 250 to 300 degrees.

Place the chicken in the smoker and close door. Adjust the vents to keep the cooking temperature between 250 and 300 degrees. Cook the chicken until a meat thermometer inserted into the thickest part of the breast reaches 165 to 170 degrees. Remove the chicken from the smoker and place on a platter. Let the chicken stand for 20 minutes, then carve and serve.

Serves 4 to 6.

1 cup kosher salt, plus more for sprinkling

½ cup sugar

1 cup fresh basil leaves

2 tablespoons peppercorns

½ cup chopped chives

½ lemon

1 gallon water

1 (6-pound) whole chicken

Freshly cracked black pepper

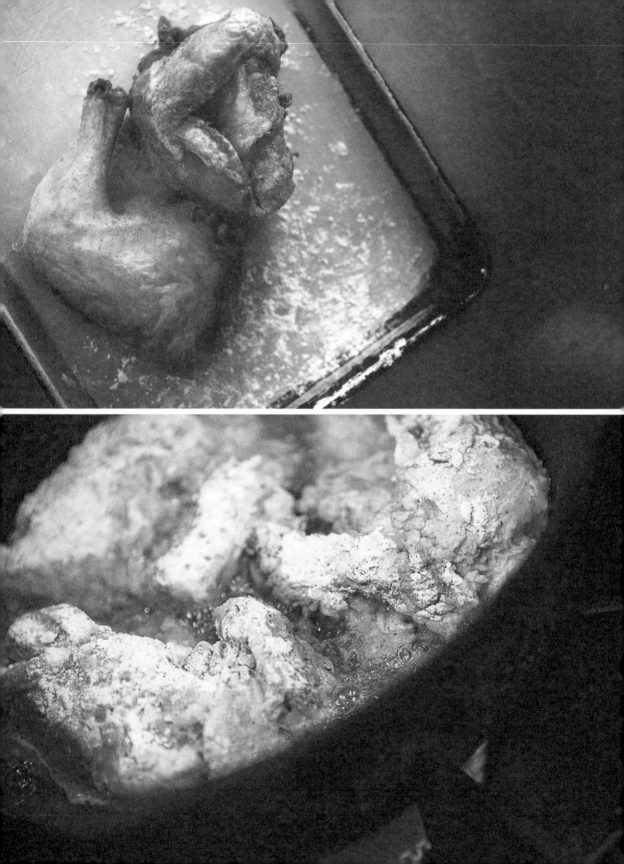

NORTH CAROLINA

North Carolina always surprises me with its diversity. Its landscape varies, just as its people do, across the state. From the mountains and new-age hipsters in the west of the state, to the piedmont plateau and down-home country folk in the central region, to the outer banks beaches and the tidewater and surfing crew, North Carolina has plenty to offer any traveler. Because of its topographical variety, North Carolina has a broad range of climate conditions and more than 400 types of soil, leading its farmers and agricultural business to grow a wide variety of crops including soybeans, corn, sweet potatoes, wheat, peanuts, blueberries, potatoes, tomatoes, and cucumbers.

With 20 percent of the state employed by the agricultural industry, North Carolinians know their meats and veggies. As I cruised across the state, I was surprised and intrigued by the variable preparations and food styles. The coastal areas have a completely different take on fried chicken than the mountain dwellers, although both had their positive attributes. Throughout the state, though, the differences were bound together with the common thread of Southern hospitality.

When I think of North Carolina, I can't help but think of the characters Andy Griffith, Barney Fife, and Aunt Bee from the popular *Andy Griffith Show* that ran from 1960 to 1968 in first-runs and still appears occasionally as reruns. Maybe that's because Andy Griffith was a native North Carolinian, and he modeled Mayberry after his very own hometown of Mount Airy. Or maybe it's because the characters I encountered along the way drew me back to that setting of hometown humility and goodwill, with a touch of humor thrown in for good measure. Who knows? I do know that this state must be doing something right when it comes to raising its children. The list of people who grew up here and have made a mark on the landscape of this country or even the world includes Christian evangelist Billy Graham, sports journalist Howard Cosell, singer Roberta Flack, and writer O. Henry.

Just as the state boasts several famous characters, known for their individual talents, it also boasts several delicious meat and three restaurants that are worthy of national and maybe even international recognition. North Carolina for me is such a wonderful destination, rich in experiences. It's become a sort of new home away from home. I've made some incredible friends during my journey who are more like family now. We have broken bread together and shared stories. The glue that binds these ten

North Carolina restaurants together is the labor of love that the owners and staff engage in to make their customers feel like family.

The basis of Southern food, in general, and meat and three food, specifically, is simple food and regional ingredients prepared well and rich with love. Southern food is possibly this country's first authentic cuisine. As I traveled the North Carolina landscape, this is exactly what I encountered—simple, authentic food with fresh, regional ingredients and people willing to dole out a healthy helping of love with their black-eyed peas. The Southern recipes I know and love most are the recipes I can imagine being prepared for dinner several hundred years ago, with the same care and appreciation for food and family and the same gratitude for time spent together.

With an ever-changing food landscape tailored to the fickle consumer, it's hard to find time-tested restaurants that continue to preserve the legacy of those who have gone before them. The restaurants in North Carolina and throughout this book stay true to the authenticity and traditions of the Southern meat and three restaurants. The food style of meat and three restaurants hasn't been ignored, but has been awarded respect and has been left alone to continue on its path of being original and spontaneous.

Charlotte Café

Charlotte, North Carolina

The mission of owners Mary and Jim Roupas of the Charlotte Café is to bring new, healthier, and better flavors to the community by opening great restaurants. And they've certainly been successful at it. Mary and Jim have opened fourteen restaurants in the city. The Charlotte Café is just one, and like the couple's other restaurants, this place has a personality and clientele all its own. The original restaurant was called Deli Town of Park Road. It was simple, serving sandwiches and salads with heavy local clientele, but the owners felt the name of the restaurant limited their abilities to serve the type of food they really wanted to feed to the community of Charlotte. Mary explained that they took notice of their customers and felt that demand seemed to tilt more toward healthy plate lunches, country breakfasts, and meat and three dinners. So with many changes behind the scenes, the Deli was quickly transformed into the Charlotte Café. Instead of just renaming the restaurant, the husband and wife restaurateurs gave the joint a facelift. The food philosophy was to be simple, as Mary explains, fresh, local when available, and healthful recipes.

I enjoyed the time I spent with Mary chatting about the restaurant and sharing our memories of food, family, and the South. However, it was the stories of some of the staff that painted a picture for me of the true Southern meat and three café. One server referred to the dining room at certain times of the day as "God's waiting room." She describes how the older guests typically congregate for a few hours in the late afternoon to eat an early dinner. She told a story of how one elderly regular called her to the table and asked if she would bring a paper sack and meet her near the restrooms. However odd she found the request to be, she met the customer at the door of the restaurant's bathrooms. Just when she wasn't sure what could possibly happen next, the little old lady reached through the slight opening in the door and handed her a girdle. The elderly customer whispered through the door that it needed to come off if she wanted to enjoy dessert.

The Charlotte Café exceeds expectations of food and service, and the personalities I encountered there are the cherry on top of a sundae for a well-rounded experience. My favorite quality of this place is the delicate, uncomplicated way that the kitchen treats fish. It's a perfect and timeless technique to cook the flaky white flounder, a true homage to Southern cooking that shows respect by using what's available and keeping the flavors clean. I suggest trying it in a cast-iron skillet. It feels more authentic, and the crust develops more evenly.

2 tablespoons cold butter, divided

1 large egg

1 tablespoon water

½ cup crushed saltine crackers

2 (6-ounce) fresh flounder fillets, cleaned and boned

Salt and pepper to taste

BROWN BUTTER PAN-FRIED CAROLINA FLOUNDER

Place 1 tablespoon of the butter in a cast-iron skillet and melt over medium-high heat.

In a small bowl whisk the egg and water. Place the cracker crumbs in another small bowl. Dredge the fish fillets in the egg mixture, moistening both sides. Then dredge the fillets in the crackers. Add the fillets to the hot butter and cook until golden brown on one side, about 3 ½ minutes. Flip the fillets and add the remaining 1 tablespoon butter to the pan. Cook until golden brown, about 3 ½ minutes. Remove the fillets from the pan and place on a platter. Sprinkle with salt and pepper.

Serves 2.

The King's Kitchen

Charlotte, North Carolina

The King's Kitchen in Charlotte is not just a restaurant; it plays a vital part in caring for the homeless and teaching skills to the unemployed. The restaurant was founded on the philosophy of great food, but was also established to raise awareness and money for the homeless, poor, and those recovering from substance abuse. Like most selfless acts, the idea took off, and with the community's support, chef-owner Jim Noble's business is thriving. Jim has developed a learning-on-the-job program called the discipleship program that leads participants toward full-time employment. The restaurant is beautiful and the mission is amazing, with 100 percent of the profits going to feed the homeless in the Charlotte area.

With his love for food and people, Jim has found success in many arenas and added other restaurants to his restaurant group. His food standards, support of the community with faith-based principles, delicious cooking, and donations of profits have inspired many other authentic mission-based restaurants to follow suit.

Jim learned the delicate art of culinary skills by working in a pretty demanding culinary atmosphere: the pizza station at Pizza Hut. Okay, so I exaggerated a touch, but he did work at Pizza Hut so he could live near the beach for a few summers and surf. In 1982, he traveled to Napa, California, and fell in love with the local, fresh, Mediterranean-style foods being prepared. He was able to combine what he had learned in California with what he remembered about growing up in the South. This experience created a flair for fresh, local, and sustainable foods prepared with French techniques, but using Southern ingredients and family recipes. Growing up in the South, Jim recalls that the Noble family had a garden, and in full season the dinner table

would be peppered with as many as fourteen different vegetable dishes. When he entered the restaurant business back in North Carolina, he had the chance to show his creativity on his own turf. Jim's ability in the kitchen was real and he was determined to make his mark. He liked the notion of meat and three restaurants, but the old-school recipes were not speaking Jim's food language. He wanted fresh, meaningful, well-thought, and courageous dishes.

The recipe I've chosen to represent King's Kitchen is reminiscent of what Jim is accomplishing: simple, elegant, courageous, humble, and tasty food. I love the idea that one cast-iron pan, some corn, butter, and salt can create a mouth memory that will forever replace the flavor you once thought of as corn. This fried corn is so simple and delicious anyone can make it, but it often gets overlooked because it's such a no-brainer. The layers of flavors and textures you develop from cooking corn in this manner are fantastic, crunchy, soft, toasted, and buttery. Jim has so many other incredible dishes at the restaurant. If I hadn't chosen corn, I may have been won over by Aunt Beaut's Fried Chicken. It's a Sunday-only tradition at King's Kitchen and worth the trip.

PAN-FRIED CORN

1 tablespoon lard

3 cups fresh corn kernels (about 6 medium ears)

1 tablespoon butter

Pinch of salt and pepper

Place the lard in a large cast-iron skillet and heat over medium-high until just before smoking point. Add the corn and spread it in the pan. Cook undisturbed to allow the bottom layer of corn to slightly brown. Once the bottom layer of corn is brown, add the butter, salt, and pepper and stir until the butter is melted and fully incorporated. Serve hot.

Serves 4.

Lupie's Café

Charlotte, North Carolina

Lupie's Café in Charlotte feeds, employs, and supports the community, breathing life and soul into the city it occupies. This is big picture stuff, not just profit-hungry entrepreneurial ideas, but selfless standards that breed success by putting other people first.

Owner Lupie Duran has been working her entire life serving other people. It wasn't easy, but she always made the best of her circumstances. She gained her initial cooking experience as a child, cooking for her siblings, and she remembers running back and forth to her mother, who was sick in bed, to ask her specific questions about each recipe. When her mother's illness progressed, she decided that placing the children in an orphanage would provide the structure and stability that her young children needed. Although for most children this sounds like the worst possible scenario, Lupie looks back on her time at the church-operated orphanage with gratitude and fondness. She remembers Willie Mae who worked in the orphanage kitchen and first taught Lupie how to cook professionally and for the masses.

As an adult, Lupie went on to work in professional restaurant kitchens. She blended surprisingly well with the all-male cooking staffs she frequently encountered. They loved her proven abilities in the kitchen, her sharp tongue, and her high tolerance for after-shift drinking. It is during this period of her life that Lupie found her real passion in cooking—soups and sauces. She learned how to master the techniques from a dedicated Swiss master chef that cooked in a local restaurant. She studied the process of building flavors and developing viscosity when cooking liquid-based recipes.

In June 1987 Lupie put all that training to good use and opened Lupie's Café. Her business quickly began thriving, and within the first five years, she doubled the size of the restaurant's dining room with a new addition. Now Lupie says she keeps it simple. However, for her, simple involves two locations and a scratch kitchen that feeds hundreds of hungry Southerners each day. Still, with a belly full of fire for cooking, she hangs her hat on her proven ability with tasty soups, stews, chilis, and sauces. Lupie's Café always has a full rotating seasonal meat and three menu.

As a Southern transplant, I'm a bit of a sucker for chicken and dumplings. I think it's the starchy thing happening on the plate— the creamy roux-based sauce, the roasted vegetables, and the slow-cooked chicken. And, of course, the gooier the better when it comes to dumplings, and bite by bite Lupie's chicken and dumpling dish is a true winner. Her study of sauces, soups, and stews really stands out in this Southern favorite.

CHICKEN AND DUMPLINGS

Wash the chicken and place in a large pot. Cover with water and add the bay leaves. Sprinkle with some of the salt and pepper and add the butter to the water. Bring to a full boil over medium-high heat and cook, uncovered, until the chicken is fully cooked, 45 minutes to 1 hour.

Remove the chicken from the pot and let cool slightly. Discard the bay leaves. When the chicken has cooled, pick the meat from the bones and return the chicken meat to the broth.

In a large bowl, mix the oil, eggs, water, and 1 teaspoon salt. Add the flour, blending it with a fork or whisk. Stir gently, only long enough for the ingredients to be fully incorporated.

Empty the dough out onto a floured work surface. Divide the dough in half. Roll out one piece of the dough to 1/2-inch thick. Slice the dough into 1/2 x 1-inch strips. Repeat with the remaining dough.

Bring the broth and chicken back to a boil over medium-high heat. Drop the dumpling strips into the boiling stock. Boil for 10 minutes, uncovered, until the dumplings are puffy and floating. Gently stir occasionally to prevent sticking. Serve with extra black pepper and hot sauce.

Serves 8.

1 (3- to 4-pound) whole chicken

5 bay leaves

1 teaspoon salt, plus more for sprinkling, divided

Freshly cracked black pepper

4 to 6 tablespoons butter

1 cup vegetable oil

2 large eggs

3/4 cup water

3 1/4 cups all-purpose flour

Hot sauce to taste

Mama Dip's

Chapel Hill, North Carolina

Mama Dip's is a local fixture and true iconic Southern restaurant in Chapel Hill. The restaurant opened thirty-seven years ago, but the story behind it starts long before Mama Dip's served its first customer.

The name comes from a childhood nickname given to Mildred Cotton Council. As a child, Mildred's height and arm length were greater than the other children in her town, and this advantage allowed her to dip into the bottom of a rain barrel without much effort. The nickname stuck, and so has her reputation for cooking amazing, authentic Southern food. In the late 1940s, Mildred started honing her cooking craft and developing recipes for what eventually would become the menu at her restaurant. She worked as a family cook and later became a cook for a busy local coffee and breakfast shop. But it wasn't until the late 1950s, when she and her late mother-in-law opened a tiny catering kitchen, that Mildred had the space and time to test, refine, and develop recipes and cooking techniques for a serious following of hungry customers in Chapel Hill. When the catering kitchen was about to burst, she knew the timing was right for her to take a leap of faith. So with forty dollars of food purchases, a lease on a building, and twenty-four bucks in the register for change, Mama Dip's opened for business.

The food and atmosphere at Mama Dip's restaurant are successful because they are simple and done well. Consistency and giving the customer what the customer craves are the tenets that rule.

When I ate at this Southern gem and reviewed the menu, I wanted to base my food selection on the difficulty of technique and recipe. I knew Mildred excelled at fried chicken, slaw, beans, greens, and most Southern things, but the delicate handling of a temperamental ingredient like okra, well, that takes true talent.

My kids don't enjoy okra, but I do. I like the qualities it brings to the plate. I'm not a textural eater, so slippery, slimy, crunchy, or smooth, I savor them all. However, what I don't enjoy is when the ingredient has one of those textural characteristics because it's been either misused or poorly cooked. Mama Dip's cooks fried okra the way I'd imagine okra would describe itself if it was creating a profile for an online dating site. It's brilliant, buttery, and creamy, but not slimy, with acidic and savory notes and a superb crunch power.

I like Mama Dip's for many reasons. I like the history, and I love that Mildred still works at the restaurant even in her eighties. Her labor of love, her regimen, and her contribution to a beautiful community have made this little meat and three restaurant a star.

FRIED OKRA

Wash the okra and dry thoroughly. Trim off the ends and cut the okra into ½-inch rounds. In a large bowl beat the eggs and hot sauce. Add the okra to the egg mixture and stir to coat. In a shallow dish, combine the cornmeal, salt, and cayenne. Dredge the okra pieces through the cornmeal mixture.

Pour 2 inches of the oil into a deep skillet. Heat the oil to 350 to 360 degrees. Add the okra in small batches and fry until golden brown, 4 to 6 minutes. Frying in batches will keep the oil from cooling down. Transfer the okra to a paper towel–lined plate to drain. Serve immediately.

Serves 6 to 8.

2 pounds fresh okra

4 large eggs

6 to 10 dashes hot pepper sauce

2 cups cornmeal

1 teaspoon salt

1 teaspoon cayenne pepper

Canola oil for deep-frying

Old Richmond Grill

Pfafftown, North Carolina

I always imagine the perfect Southern food experience to include an over-loaded menu, a bird's-eye view into the kitchen from my counter seat complete with swivel stool, and counter service only. The Old Richmond Grill, in business in Pfafftown since 1955, meets all of my criteria and also manages to serve super delicious food. The restaurant has changed hands a few times over the last sixty years, but the new owner, Chris Sostaita, and family are hitting a home run with food, service, and community support. Chris and his family passed by the restaurant time after time for more than twenty years, always thinking to themselves, if that restaurant ever became available, we would hop on the chance to buy it. In 2012 Chris got his chance. The owners of the Old Richmond Grill were retiring, and Chris attended church with the property owner, who happened to know full well that Chris was interested. The Sostaita family took the leap and haven't looked back since.

I hear the passion and determination in Chris's voice as he describes the operations of his new business. He is excited, faithful, and determined. Chris's wife and children stop by each morning on the way to school and work for a quick breakfast and to say hi to dad as he operates the grill for a busy breakfast service. While hospitality is a common goal in the restaurant business, at the Old Richmond Grill, it's different, more personal. Chris dreamed of buying the business for years, thinking through the process endless times, and talking through how or what he might do differently if he were able to take ownership. Chris's story mirrors a romance, and through that I see real dedication, conviction, and the beautiful result of amazing country food.

The food is straightforward Southern cooking, with a few community favorites. I chose the community favorite, Fried Chicken Bacon Ranch Po' Boy, because it's so different from what was offered at the other restaurants I visited while traveling. It doesn't hurt that it's also delicious. And lucky you, Chris has shared the recipe. You may be wondering how that can be called a meat and three entrée. Well first, there are no rules, and it's my book, and second, it's so ridiculously tasty, with truly familiar Southern flair. It's a well-prepared sandwich. If you visit the Old Richmond Grill, tell Chris if he adds two or three more menu items like this, I may just move to town.

Fried Chicken Bacon Ranch Po'Boy (page 174)

Chicken

2 cups corn oil

2 cups all-purpose flour

2 cups semolina flour

Cajun seasoning

2 (12-ounce) cans beer

2 pounds chicken tenders

Assembly

1 (8- to 10-ounce) crusty
French bread loaf

4 tablespoons ranch
dressing

1 tomato, sliced ¼-inch
thick

1 cup shredded lettuce

6 slices thick-cut bacon,
crisply cooked

2 tablespoons pickle slices

FRIED CHICKEN BACON RANCH PO' BOY

Pour the oil into a large, deep skillet and heat over medium-high until the oil reaches 350 degrees.

In a large bowl, mix the flour, semolina, and Cajun seasoning. Add the beer and stir until a batter forms. Add the chicken and stir until the chicken is well coated. Transfer the chicken tenders, a few at a time, to the hot oil and fry until golden brown, 6 to 8 minutes.

To assemble the sandwich, cut a slit in the bread lengthwise and open the bread. Spread the ranch dressing on both cut sides. Place the sliced tomatoes on the bottom piece of bread and top them with the lettuce and the fried chicken. Add the bacon and pickles. Fold the bread top over the sandwich to close. Cut the sandwich into 4 pieces.

Serves 4.

Smoky Mountain Diner

Hot Springs, North Carolina

The Smoky Mountain Diner has a huge personality. That may be a strange thing to say about a restaurant, but after hearing the stories behind this local gem, I really don't think there's another way to put it. The restaurant lives in an old tomato-packing house that provides a perfect backdrop to this wonderful Southern meat and three. As Genia Hayes-Peterson, the owner-manager, explains, she was raised to respect Southern hospitality, and that's what her restaurant delivers day in and day out. The locals may be found in the dining room two or three times a day, and Genia has become the community favorite by keeping her café doors open on all holidays. The holiday season is for family, and at the Smoky Mountain Diner, the customers are family. Genia tries to meet the needs of her community, and every Thursday is seniors' day with one-price plates. If seniors in the community can't afford a one-price plate, it's on the house. The sense I get when hearing about the business and how Genia operates it is that this is her faith-based way of giving people God through good food. She admits she sometimes tries to slide in some healthier options on the menu, but the locals typically crave the delicious Southern fare that put Genia's little diner on the map.

From how Genia tells it, learning to cook from her "Mammaw" was harder than getting a culinary degree, but those lessons prepared her for the balancing act between life outside her restaurant and life in her kitchen. The way she developed her skills is important to her story and keeps Genia grounded as her business grows. Her customers can't get enough of the meatloaf or her pan-fried chicken, truly a labor of love. And when you serve several hundred people a day—well, you get the picture. My favorite on her menu, though, is a true Southern treat—Mammaw's Pepper Jelly. If you're in the South and see pepper jelly, buy it. It's part pickle, part jelly, sometimes sweet and always a little spicy. The pepper jelly Mammaw perfected is smooth and tasty and leaves you craving more. Now I just need the recipe. Here's another Southern staple that you can make at home. Use it to spice up most anything coming out of your kitchen.

HOT PEPPER RELISH

9 cups minced hot peppers, seeds and veins removed

6 tablespoons canning and pickling salt

4 cups sugar

1 cup water

5 cups cider vinegar

In a large skillet or Dutch oven over medium heat, add all the peppers and cook them until they begin to sweat. Add the salt and cook, stirring, for 5 minutes. Add the sugar and cook until it begins to caramelize, stirring constantly to allow for even cooking. Add the water and vinegar, and cook, scraping the bottom of the pan to release any browned bits. Bring the entire mixture to a full boil and cook until the liquid is reduced by half. Remove from the heat and let cool. Store in the refrigerator.

Serves 8.

NOTE: In this relish, try using Anaheim peppers, jalapeño peppers, and Bulgarian carrot peppers. Mix in some bell peppers for the less spicy varietal and to add a touch of savory. Canning and pickling salt is pure salt that has not been packaged with anti-caking ingredients, which can cause foods to get cloudy and dark.

Stax's Original Restaurant

Greenville, North Carolina

The look and feel of a restaurant housed in an old pharmacy is remarkable. Stax's Original Restaurant in Greenville is original in so many ways—from paying at the counter, to the handwritten checks, to waitresses who have worked there for thirty-plus years. Not many changes have happened here. But why change something that works so well and is loved by many? From talking about the business with owners Michael and Nick Stathakis, you quickly figure out that Stax's runs like a well-oiled machine and feeds the masses day in and day out. If you grew up in Greenville and had a last name of Stathakis, chances are that your day started at five o'clock in the morning at Stax's Original, and you worked the position of "whatever it takes." Being a restaurant manager and owner means working as a counselor, cashier, bank, busboy, cook, waiter, friend, and referee. But the many hats are part of the gig, and these guys love their job. There is a philosophy at Stax's Original—"it's about the customer"—but as their granddad told them, "If the customer is always right, you're in the wrong business."

Stax's Original boasts big dishes and big flavors, featuring loads of original recipes and family dishes. Basically a meat and three, the restaurant encourages the guests to choose their protein and then pick their veggies. And mac 'n' cheese has maintained a place on the vegetable menu for decades. Is it a vegetable or a pasta—who knows? Frankly, I don't care. I just admire the courage that it took for someone at some point to add this cheesy pasta favorite to the veggie menu in a way that simply made sense to everyone.

Inside, you can see how the space was transformed from a pharmacy to a diner. In the early days, the restaurant offered only counter service. The four counters with nine seats each were popular with the locals because the arrangement encouraged conversation. Fresh from the mill, cotton field, or local professional office, the crowd that gathered at Stax's Original was and is as diverse as the menu.

You can't have a name like Stathakis and exclude an authentic gyro from your small-town restaurant. All the food is tasty and well prepared by a family that loves food, people, and the restaurant business itself. But I've chosen Stax's mac 'n' cheese to include here. The taste, consistency, and flawlessly cooked pasta won my vote. Stax's mac 'n' cheese is as Southern as it gets, even if it hails from a Greek diner.

MAC 'N' CHEESE

2 cups whole milk

1 ¼ teaspoons dry mustard

3 teaspoons granulated garlic

1 teaspoon salt

½ teaspoon pepper

Pinch of freshly grated nutmeg

Pinch of cayenne pepper

2 pounds shredded extra-sharp Cheddar cheese

1 ½ cups grated Parmesan cheese

1 pound elbow pasta

Preheat oven to 350 degrees.

Place the milk, dry mustard, granulated garlic, salt, pepper, nutmeg, and cayenne in a blender jar and process until smooth and creamy.

Pour the milk mixture into a large bowl and add half the Cheddar and Parmesan cheeses. Mix well. Add the dry pasta and fold all the ingredients together.

Pour the pasta mixture into a 9 x 13-inch baking dish, top with the remaining cheese, and cover with foil. Bake for 30 minutes. Before serving allow the mac 'n' cheese to cool to room temperature. This will allow the fats to redistribute back into the casserole.

Serves 6.

The Derby Restaurant

Mount Airy, North Carolina

n 1937 America took great pride in the opening of the Golden Gate Bridge, a new home was priced to sell at $4,100, Amelia Earhart mysteriously disappeared while flying over the Pacific, gas was a whopping ten cents a gallon, and if you lived anywhere near Mount Airy, you likely were getting ready to meet friends for supper at The Derby Cottage. The original structure was a small, white house, with location, location, location on the mind of founder James Weldon Pell Sr. He built his first restaurant at a fork in the road of the tiny town of Mount Airy. With sandwiches and hotdogs as the primary focus of early menus, James saw the success he could have and was determined to grow his family business.

Nearly ten years after he'd opened the doors, he had an idea to provide home cooking, conveniently, and at fair prices. He built a big

round building in the center of town, with a separate building shaped like a derby hat right in the front. The "hat," as it would be referred to by its customers, offered ice cream and gas and was similar to a drive-in restaurant: you park, eat, and hang out. The larger, semicircular structure was the main restaurant that eventually became a full-service sit-down meat and three restaurant. The business was doing well, and James thought it would be an opportunity for his son to learn the family business. Carolina summers are hot, and he'd had just about enough of working as a carhop. He quickly elected his son, James W. Pell Jr. (Jimmy), to manage the "hat" for the season. The story often told at the restaurant goes something like this: "We didn't make any money, the product was always going missing and James, Jr., gained fifty pounds in one summer."

Jimmy finally took over operating The Derby, at a profit, when his father passed away in 1973. At that time, Jimmy had a son of his own, James Pell III (Jimbo). At ten years old, Jimbo was bussing tables and clearing plates. He remembers that he hated the chore almost as much as the spankings he received if he refused to help. He soon progressed from clearing and cleaning to washing dishes and then found his comfort zone as a short-order cook. After college, Jimbo worked at The Derby again, but by then the family owned two locations, and he and his father split the operational

stories to determine the level of bonding happening over lunch. I thought he would just cave in and cough it up, but it took some convincing. The Derby Restaurant has offered this meatloaf recipe for fifty-two years, and the same person, now in her eighties, has prepared it every day since it first appeared on the menu.

You know you've met a true original when they share stories and experiences with such clarity that you can actually picture yourself having an ice cream with an overweight high-school carhop. I laughed out loud at some of the stories Jimbo told. What I encountered is what every customer has encountered every day for the last seventy-seven years—a genuine, authentic, caring person. The Derby is a titan, a success over three generations and through evolving food tastes. If you're in the neighborhood near Mount Airy, The Derby Restaurant is my choice for a ridiculously delicious meatloaf. I'll bet if you make a visit, you will also make some new friends.

duties. In 1999 when Jimmy retired, Jimbo purchased the sixty-two-year-old restaurant from his father, closed the second location, and decided to focus on the original semicircular building—The Derby.

With a core of meat and three offerings, the menu specials change daily, with a rotation of local favorites and family recipes. Over three generations, this family progressed from hotdogs, gas, and ice-cream to steaks, burgers, chops, and salads. The business evolved as the town evolved; the Pell family sensed a need for full service and delivered, and the community embraced it.

This recipe wasn't as easy to get as I imagined. I was gauging Jimbo as we shared

THE DERBY MEATLOAF

In a large bowl mix together the beef, pancake mix, ketchup, onion, bell pepper, cornflakes, eggs, and salt. Do not use a mixer. Divide in half. Shape two loaves, placing each loaf in a 9 x 13-inch baking dish, and refrigerate for 30 minutes.

Preheat the oven to 350 degrees.

Remove the meatloaves from the refrigerator and cover with aluminum foil. Bake for 30 to 40 minutes or until a meat thermometer inserted into the center reaches 155 degrees.

Uncover the meatloaves, drain any excess fat drippings from the pan, and smear a thin layer of ketchup on top of the loaves. Return the pan to the oven and cook, uncovered, for 10 minutes, or until lightly browned.

Serves 12 to 15.

5 pounds ground beef (80 percent lean)

¾ pound pancake mix

3 cups ketchup, plus more for topping

½ cup finely chopped onion

¼ cup finely chopped green bell pepper

¼ (18-ounce) box corn flakes

5 eggs

1 tablespoon salt

Toot-n-Tell

Garner, North Carolina

Sixty-eight years ago, Mary Ann Sparkman's stepfather purchased a restaurant that may be the first fast-food drive-through restaurant. The old military barracks building was sandwiched between train tracks and a graveyard. Mary Ann, the owner-operator of the restaurant, explains the name behind the interesting little meat and three joint. The customers were able to pull up, toot their horn, and tell the attendant their orders.

In the beginning Toot-n-Tell offered simple fare. As she gives me the roster of menu items from 1968, the year she and her husband, Bill, became the owners, the "infrared sandwich" intrigues me. The early microwave was a popular and convenient appliance for restaurateurs who needed to deliver hot food to the hard-working community. The early microwave used infrared waves to warm the food. Ham and cheese on white bread was fine, but when it was served as the "infrared sandwich," all melted, gooey, and warm, it was perfect.

Mary Ann admits, like any small family-owned business owner, the best of times for her and the family may not have always been the easiest. She says that sometimes it was tough raising her three children in what she refers to as "Toot-n-Tell-University," but she took her limited kitchen abilities and grew her small business into a meat and three empire, now serving as many as two hundred people a day. Some of the regular TNT (Toot-N-Tell) customers eat three meals a day in her dining room. She is very humble and explains, "We make some money, but we are not setting the world on fire." With a staff that's been with her since the beginning, consistency is the standard.

Mary Ann and the TNT staff found the secret to my heart with their chocolate pie and shared the recipe with me. It takes skill to make, and if you prepare fresh in-house desserts everyday by the dozens to feed two hundred-plus regular guests, well, it takes courage too.

CHOCOLATE PIE

Preheat the oven to 400 degrees.

On a lightly floured surface, roll the pie dough to a 13-inch circle. Place in a 9-inch pie pan, crimping the edges of the dough, and pricking the bottom with a fork in several places. Refrigerate for 30 minutes. Place a sheet of parchment on top of the crust and place pie weights on the paper. Bake the crust for 10 minutes. Remove from the oven, and remove the paper and weights. Return the crust to the oven and continue baking until golden brown, about 15 minutes. Remove from the oven and let cool completely.

Place the sugar, flour, and cocoa in a saucepan. In a medium bowl, mix the milk and egg yolks until well incorporated. Pour the milk mixture into the saucepan and stir well. Cook over medium heat, constantly stirring, until thickened, 8 to 10 minutes. Remove from the heat and stir in the butter and vanilla extract. Pour the chocolate mixture into the piecrust. Refrigerate until cool and firm.

Serves 8.

Pie dough for 1 (9-inch) piecrust, chilled

1 cup sugar

3 tablespoons all-purpose flour

3 tablespoons cocoa powder

1 cup whole milk

3 large egg yolks, beaten

¼ cup (½ stick) butter

2 teaspoons vanilla extract

Wallburg Diner

Winston-Salem, North Carolina

We need to pause and recognize how big a deal it is that I've nominated the Wallburg Diner in Winston-Salem for having some of the best fried chicken in the South. Southerners are very particular about fried chicken, so this is kind of a big move as I have only one spot for fried chicken in the entire book. So first, be sure to mark your map and make sure it's Monday, because that's fried chicken day at the Wallburg Diner. If you miss the day, no worries. Everything there is good.

This restaurant lives in an old cinder-block house situated across from the elementary school and next door to the post office. The entire made-from-scratch menu is created daily, which is a true commitment, considering the number of guests the Wallburg Diner serves each day. Owner Judy Whitaker shares stories of growing up and learning to cook from her mother. According to Judy, her mother had the

town convinced that she was the best thing since sliced bread to come to a supper table, or maybe even that she invented it. Even though her mother passed away a few years ago, Judy admits that she still grabs for the phone to call mom for recipe advice or directions.

The community has supported Judy's restaurant since the beginning, with regulars waiting at the door every morning at five o'clock. She explains that her regulars are so consistent that if they didn't show up on time, she might just send out a search party. The stories the regulars and the staff at the Wallburg Diner tell match perfectly the image of a small Southern town. Think of a Norman Rockwell painting depicting each detail and giving life and character to someone you don't even know. Better yet, bypass the typecast images you may have just come up with, and pack up the car, loosen your belt, and be prepared for life-altering Southern food and Southern people.

The food at the Wallburg Diner is traditional but relevant with a healthy dose of character. The fried chicken stole my heart. To kick off its preparation, the quarter bird gets a healthy one-hour spa treatment in a salt-water bath.

FRIED CHICKEN

6 quarts water

3 cups plus 1 tablespoon salt, plus more for sprinkling

4 cups sugar

2 tablespoons black peppercorns

6 cups ice

8 pounds chicken quarters

1 gallon buttermilk

3 cups all-purpose flour

½ tablespoon pepper, plus more for sprinkling

Vegetable oil for frying

Mix the water, 3 cups of the salt, sugar, and peppercorns in a large container. Stir well to dissolve the sugar and salt. Add the ice and chicken and let the chicken marinate for 1 hour.

After marinating the chicken, remove it from the brine and submerge it in the buttermilk. Let stand for 1 hour.

Combine the flour, remaining 1 tablespoon salt, and pepper. Remove the chicken pieces from the buttermilk, letting excess buttermilk drain back into the bowl. Dredge each piece in the seasoned flour, pressing the flour to adhere.

Pour 3 inches of the vegetable oil into a large, deep skillet. Heat the oil over medium-high to 325 degrees. Cook the chicken in small batches until golden brown, about 25 minutes. Too many pieces in the oil will reduce the oil temperature and create soggy chicken.

Once the chicken is fully cooked, place it on a paper towel–lined platter and sprinkle with salt and pepper.

Serves 16.

SOUTH CAROLINA

There is definitely something to love and admire about a state whose motto is "While I breathe, I hope." There are no defeatist attitudes in South Carolina, that's for sure. I saw the spirit of this motto alive and well in the restaurateurs and managers I met during my culinary journey through the state. The people of South Carolina have always been survivors. During colonial times, they were leaders in the resistance to the Stamp Act, encouraging the colonies to speak out against taxation from England not approved by local government. South Carolinians are not prone to step down from a fight. They were the first state to secede from the Union at the start of the Civil War and the site of the first shots fired during the war. This fighting spirit helped develop the strong leadership found in the native-born civil rights leader Jesse Jackson.

When the people of South Carolina believe in something, they back it wholeheartedly and with a belly full of passion. I encountered this mindset as I ate my way across the state. The communities I visited supported the local businesses by frequenting these establishments sometimes daily. The restaurants reciprocated by supporting their communities with good, home-cooked meals. The food I encountered was a labor of love, deep in history, and rich in flavors. The state has soul; and if you don't believe me, just ask the "Godfather of Soul" himself, native South Carolinian singer James Brown.

The characters I met as I traveled from the mountains of western South Carolina, to the midlands and low-country in the central region, to the eastern coast had one thing in common: a passion for good food and good people. The restaurants I visited were as varied as the landscape, and I never wanted for variety of characters or flavors. The owners and the stories of how they had progressed with the times often touched me.

At Wade's in Spartanburg, the owner has met the needs of his community even as the community has changed and adjusted. When industry left town, Wade Lindsey didn't throw in the towel or grumble about the economic pitfalls. He shifted gears and met his fellow townspeople where they were and where they needed him, providing them with a family-friendly meat and three restaurant. Because of his strength and commitment to the community, Wade's restaurant stands firm today. At Nigel's Good Food in North Charleston, this flexibility comes through in a different way, with the chef-owner showing how the old can become new again with a little thought and reinvention. Nigel Drayton takes pride in knowing the history of the food of his region

and finding a new way to reveal that history to present-day patrons. Rather than shying away from the state's past as a slave state, he dug in deep to find out how that history has shaped the food culture of the region and works to enrich his customers by not only feeding their bellies, but also by providing some historical sustenance to their minds.

When I talked to the owner-operators of the meat and three restaurants in this state, I couldn't help but get caught up in their sentiments. Their attitude of doing what it takes to get the job done and to keep the customer happy is a true sign of Southern hospitality and determination. The food is good, the people are warm, and if you have a hankering for bellyaching, this probably isn't the place for you. But if you're like me, and you appreciate the spirit of a people who keep moving forward, no matter which way the tide is pulling them, then you will enjoy your travels through South Carolina, and I promise you will have some great meals along the way.

Martha Lou's Kitchen

Charleston, South Carolina

What could possibly be unique about Martha Lou's Kitchen in Charleston? Hmm, let me think. Oh, the owner, Martha Lou Gadsden, has nine children and operates a wildly successful Southern meat and three restaurant in her "free" time. The term *overachiever* comes to mind. I can't image the hurdles of successfully raising a large family and running a business that serves breakfast, lunch, and dinner. In March 1983 Martha Lou set out on an adventure, and thirty-plus years later the consensus, with every mouth that she has fed, is that the food is as close to grandma's kitchen as anyone can recall.

Charleston's approach to Southern food is unique. It shows a certain respect for the indigenous coastal Southern ingredients, and I love it. There is a flavor in every Charleston restaurant that is distinct. Just as when you are dining in New Orleans you know you're eating from the bayou or when you're in San Francisco you're noshing on sourdough, Charleston diners recognize an undeniably authentic and memorable flavor. It's not always easy to praise a restaurant after so many newspapers and television shows have already profiled its dishes and praised the cook's raw talent in the kitchen. I was careful to do my own research. I didn't want to be a bandwagon Martha Lou fan. I wanted to formulate my own opinion. And, I have to admit, my research was enjoyable and my "findings" were delicious. Eating at Martha Lou's Kitchen was like watching an All-Star basketball team play. All the players, from the menu, to the service staff, to the kitchen staff, to the atmosphere are at the top of their game.

When you think of Southern food, you think of tradition, culture, and a respect for what was and what is. You can find this all balled up into one at Martha Lou's. I chose my dish carefully and wanted it to represent the uncomplicated nature of the entire restaurant. Pan-fried pork chop is one of those items that you hear about but don't order maybe as much as you should, and everyone has an aunt or grandma who makes a delicious family version served only on special occasions. For me, the tender, delicious, juicy, crusted chop was the perfect choice and a "best" of Martha Lou's Kitchen.

I thought I may have difficulty squeezing the recipe out of Martha Lou's hands, but because it's so simple, she had no problem sharing. None of the recipes at Martha Lou's is written down. So here is my stab at the original with final approval from my new friend Martha Lou. Using a wet batter and breading rather than the more typical dry, the recipe is easy to recreate at home if you crave the flavors of Charleston. I suggest a visit, so you can enjoy the full experience of what others have enjoyed for more than thirty years.

2 egg yolks

½ cup water at room temperature

2 cups all-purpose flour

1 tablespoon salt

½ tablespoon freshly cracked black pepper

1 teaspoon cayenne pepper

½ teaspoon onion powder

3 cups vegetable oil

4 (6-ounce) center-cut pork chops

FRIED PORK CHOPS

In a small bowl mix the egg yolks and water. Whisk in the flour, salt, pepper, cayenne, and onion powder until well incorporated.

Pour the oil into a large cast-iron skillet and heat it over medium-high to 325 degrees.

Coat each chop in the batter and slide into the hot oil. After the chops separate from the bottom of the pan, let them cook for another 3 minutes. Flip them over and cook an additional 3 minutes. Remove the pork chops from the oil and place on a paper towel–lined plate to drain and rest for 5 minutes before serving.

Serves 4.

NOTE: Martha Lou's Kitchen serves pan-fried pork chops with a delicious gravy smothering the chop—a perfect symphony of Southern flavors.

Nigel's Good Food

North Charleston, South Carolina

Chef Nigel Drayton speaks my language. He has the training, food philosophy, and skill that makes his Southern eatery, Nigel's Good Food in North Charleston, a success. It's one part meat and three and one part elevated study of culture and food roots. As a result, Nigel runs a restaurant like no other you will read about in this book. He is bridging the gap between old school and new school, country and trendy. A native-born Southerner, he is determined not just to eat the regional fare but also to understand the distinctive food flavors of his town.

The work involved in opening, operating, and maintaining a successful restaurant is hard enough, but Chef Nigel is also educating his customers and community. He wants to be free of the stereotype "soul food." But how different is soul food from Southern food in general? Are they the same? Both food styles share a lot of similar ingredients, but are there differences in styles and methods? Chef Nigel's simple answer is that soul food is typically simpler, less polished, and certainly basic in its essence. Soul food is likely to be more heavily derived from its origins with West African slaves, who used weekly rations to prepare meals, such as intestines (chitterlings), pig's feet, tripe, jowl, and other less desirable cuts from the animal. Frying the meats was a method used to encourage the tenderizing process and make the meats and textures more palatable. This would be considered true soul food. Southern food, on the other hand, may use the pricier cuts such as the chops and loins. This would be the style of food that the plantation owners preferred to eat in their own homes.

Chef Nigel is a Southern-style restaurateur who has reinvented the art of soul food. He has polished the techniques, but he respects the ingredients and where the dishes come from. His style isn't rustic or sloppy. It's elevated Southern food with soul. Each item on the menu is constructed from something old but raised up to feel new and familiar. The guy cooks great food and presents it without pretenses.

For my meal at Nigel's Good Food, I chose a dish that was a representation of all things Southern and soul and is a favorite of the majority of his customers. I didn't dare attempt to recreate the recipe with its infinite details and processes but present here an easier version that the home cook can prepare. Nigel's oyster stew is something that absolutely speaks of the South, so when you load the car and hit the road, make sure to run out of gas near Nigel's Good Food and stay for a few courses.

OYSTER STEW

1 cup (2 sticks) butter

2 cups finely chopped celery

3 tablespoons minced shallots

1 ½ quarts heavy cream

3 (12-ounce) containers fresh shucked oysters with juice

Salt and ground black pepper to taste

Pinch of cayenne pepper

Melt the butter in a large skillet over medium heat. Add the celery and shallots and cook until tender, 6 to 8 minutes. Pour the heavy cream into a large pot over medium-high heat. Pour the butter and vegetables into the cream and bring the mixture to a simmer. Add the oysters and their liquid. Season with salt, pepper, and cayenne. Stir continuously until the oysters begin to curl, 4 to 6 minutes. Cook 3 minutes longer. Remove from the heat and serve.

Serves 4.

Norma's Truck Stop

Gaffney, South Carolina

All good food may have started at a truck stop or some sort of equivalent. Think about it. Typically restaurateurs and chefs are broke and always looking for an affordable location and a way to serve people tasty food. My wife laughs at me when I travel because I always stop for gas at certain truck stops and truly enjoy the tasty food being spooned over the counter. Each of these eateries is known for a certain dish—maybe a burger, pulled pork, or potato log (a giant, fried, overly seasoned wedge of potato, kind of like a French fry for Bigfoot).

At Norma's Truck Stop in Gaffney, don't expect things to move quickly, as each order is cooked to order, and the line grows long. However, the food is definitely worth the wait. On my food adventure, half the fun of the journey is in the discovery. If every restaurant looked the same or as I think it should look, I'd be disappointed, and my belly would be half empty. Norma's is family-owned and -operated by people who pull multiple shifts just cooking good Southern food the way they know how. There are no pleasantries and no frills, but why would there be? The concept isn't muddled; it's simple and realizes its true identity. That alone is something to respect. I'm thinking I've stumbled on to something rather special at Norma's Truck Stop, and considering the size of the line, I'm not the first person to have figured that out.

As I entered Norma's Truck Stop, the customers were leaving with huge bologna burgers with cheese or beef burgers the size of small cats. The portions were a little over the top for me, but because the food is so good, I have no gripe with the big ole portions. As I perused the menu, I saw all types of tempting combos with breakfast, lunch, and in-betweens, but what caught my eye and

my nose was the steaming, sweet-smelling creamed corn.

There is an art to creamed corn. It's half pureed corn and half whole kernels, with other belt-loosening ingredients. It's so sweet it shouldn't even be considered a side or vegetable, but quite possibly belongs on the dessert menu instead. If you have slurped a bowl of Southern creamed corn, at this point your mouth is probably watering. You may even be debating if you would grab a roll or a slice of white bread to sop up the bits left in the bowl. I think I could have ordered the entire selection of starters and sides and still wanted more. Even with my hearty appetite and desperate persistence to try to get the original truck stop recipe, I have been denied, shut down, and undeniably locked out from having the secret to this tasty creamed corn. However, I have done my best to recreate this truck stop triumph.

Southern Sweet Creamed Corn (page 198)

10 ears fresh corn

1 ½ cups heavy cream

1 cup water

3 tablespoons sugar

2 tablespoons flour

Salt and freshly cracked black pepper

4 tablespoons bacon drippings

3 tablespoons butter

SOUTHERN SWEET CREAMED CORN

Cut the kernels from the ears of corn and place in a large bowl. Add the cream and water.

Mix together the sugar, flour, salt, and pepper and stir into the corn mixture.

In a large cast-iron skillet over medium-high heat add the bacon grease and butter. Add the corn mixture and reduce the heat to medium-low. Cook, stirring until it becomes creamy, for about 45 minutes.

Serves 8.

SeeWee Restaurant

Awendaw, South Carolina

See Wee Restaurant in Awendaw offers just what it promises on its sign: "Fresh Seafood and Good Home Cooking." The simplicity of the sign alone was enough evidence for me that the SeeWee Restaurant was a real food find. Meeting the customers' expectations is part of the SeeWee code. I love the concept of this coastal restaurant—it feels part Key West and part bayou. The exterior is a small house that's been transformed into a very cool local breakfast, lunch, and dinner spot. The menu focuses specifically on meat and three–style food, allowing the guests to choose their protein and then add veggies as they see fit. The inside of the SeeWee has the charm of an old grocery with shelves in one area from floor to ceiling sporting the over-stocked inventory ready for the big customer rush. Near the opposite wall is a check-out counter, complete with homemade treats for sale. The walls on the inside of the restaurant are peppered with everything from fishing poles and guns to paintings. Each item fits for some reason and makes the little eatery feel alive with character. I've eaten my way through several Southern states, and on my journey I've learned many new things about Southern food. I've met some incredible people who cook glorious food, and at the SeeWee Restaurant it's no different. If you have a love for Southern coastal food, you need to put SeeWee Restaurant at the top of your must-try list.

My food choice at SeeWee, the she-crab soup with sherry, swept me away. I'm aware that the soup isn't always available, but when you find a restaurant that nails the recipe the way SeeWee does, you'd better order it and put it in your book. It was a velvety, creamy, sea-permeated bisque, and then just when you thought the soup was already perfect, you get this splash of sherry vinegar that rounds out all the richness and creates a delicate balance of flavors. The owners and chef at SeeWee wouldn't budge when I asked for the recipe, but would this be much of an eating adventure if everyone was accommodating? I think not. I love a challenge, and because of that I'm recreating this stellar dish. This recipe should provide you with enough to share with friends, and maybe even give you an opportunity to make some new friends who will also fall in love with this sexy bowl of soup.

3 tablespoons butter

2 cups chopped green onions

1 teaspoon chopped garlic

4 tablespoons flour

2 cups white fish stock or vegetable broth

1 cup heavy cream

1 cup half-and-half

2 pounds lump crabmeat

½ tablespoon finely grated lemon peel

½ teaspoon salt

½ teaspoon white pepper

⅛ cup sherry

Chopped green onions, green part only, for garnish

Vinegar-based hot sauce, optional

SHE-CRAB SOUP WITH SHERRY VINEGAR

Melt the butter in a large pot over medium heat. Add the green onions and cook, stirring, until they are translucent, about 10 minutes. Add the garlic and cook for 4 minutes. Add the flour, whisking until well blended. Slowly add in the stock, whisking to remove any lumps. Cook until smooth, thick, and creamy. The mixture should be the consistency of chunky peanut butter.

Add the cream and half-and-half. Fold in the crabmeat. Add the lemon peel, salt, and white pepper. Simmer until all the flavors are well incorporated, about 15 minutes. Taste and adjust the seasoning. Serve in bowls with a drizzle of the sherry and green onion tops. It's also fabulous with a drop of vinegar-based hot sauce.

Serves 8.

Southern Thymes Café

Greer, South Carolina

The town of Greer is smack dab between Greenville and Spartanburg. Southern Thymes Café is situated just perfectly for the entire community of almost thirty thousand Southern souls to enjoy. Although it's relatively new, it's thriving and has scrumptious food and a stellar commitment to high-quality service. The building has housed multiple Southern-style restaurants, but originally it was a men's clothing store in the 1930s. The current owners and management group have done wonders with the business, creating a clean, unpretentious space that has been well received by the locals. The menu is straightforward and relevant. Owner-proprietor Mark Basanda is a little green in experience, but he knows good food and how to treat the customers. He has tried several menu changes and wisely measured his customers' responses to them. The standards of food and service are over the top and comparable to what you may find at a well-oiled corporate restaurant. I think this helps Mark. He may not have years of experience, but if you create a good plan and stick to it, then it's hard to fail when you're giving your customers exactly what they want—affordable, tasty Southern food three times a day and a consistent, well-thought-out menu.

During my visit, I opted for something a bit out of the ordinary. I'd been devouring plates and plates of very similar food, so I needed something different, something I hadn't eaten since I was thirteen years old at my first sleep-away camp—fried bologna. This dish isn't about just frying a piece of what we normally think of as deli meat; it's about the thickness of the slice, the quality of the meat, and the seasoning on the griddle. The fried bologna at Southern Thymes Café is salty and firm with an almost creamy interior, kind of smoky as if the heat brings a natural sweetness from the meat. It's worth ordering, and the restaurant is certainly worth supporting. Add it to your bologna bucket list if it exists, and if not, start one now.

1 teaspoon blackening
seasoning

1 tablespoon lard

4 (½-inch thick) slices
bologna

Pinch of salt and pepper

Vinegar-based hot sauce,
optional

FRIED BOLOGNA

Before cooking your bologna, sprinkle the blackening seasoning in
a cast-iron skillet. Heat the pan over medium-high heat and let the
seasoning slightly burn. Let the pan cool and wipe with a paper towel.
This will add an authentic smoky, country-fried flavor.

Place the pan over medium-high heat and add the lard. When
melted, add the bologna slices, sprinkle with salt and pepper, and cook
until evenly browned, 2 to 3 minutes per side. For additional flavor, add
hot sauce to the pan and scrape the bottom to remove any browned bits.
Serve immediately.

Serves 4.

Tommy's Country Ham House

Greenville, South Carolina

Tommy Stevenson, owner, creator, and chef of the popular Tommy's Country Ham House in Greenville, was bitten years ago by the restaurant bug. He started, as many do, in a side industry closely related to restaurants: restaurant equipment and supplies. Tommy picked up a lot of tricks and tips working so closely with restaurateurs, and he translated those valuable lessons into a wonderful iconic eatery.

When I first met Tommy, I was surprised by his dedication and passion toward meats and meat preparation. The guy is the real deal. He wakes up every day and heads to the restaurant to cut all the fresh meats for steaks, chops, chicken, and fish, and then, as if that isn't enough, he begins making multiple variations of homemade sausage. When this guy says "fresh," he means it. Menus are created daily from Tommy's hit list of customer favorites, such as fried chicken and gravy, sweet potato soufflé, peas, butter beans, and squash casserole. People have been devouring Tommy's Country Ham House food for more than thirty years, and considering this is Tommy's second career, he is anything but a slacker.

Tommy shared stories of customers and regulars and how he has fed almost every presidential candidate since the mid-1980s. When George H.W. Bush was touring the area as a presidential candidate, he and his campaign staff enjoyed lunch at Tommy's Country Ham House, occupying the entire dining room for almost three hours. Tommy says that when the team decided to exit, they were met with protesting PETA (People for the Ethical Treatment of Animals) activists dressed from head to toe in furry pink pig costumes. Once Bush's team saw that these were not friendly pigs, they escorted the president to the tour bus to head out of town. The protesters had other plans and barricaded the tour bus in the restaurant's parking lot with a dump truck full of fresh manure. Maybe it's not the most appetizing story to share over sunny-side-up eggs and black coffee, but Tommy's telling of it is certainly entertaining.

The restaurant continues to impress locals and visitors alike with dedication and high standards of quality. Tommy is living out his dream, day in and day out. He works for himself, feeds his community, and plays with food. For me and other cooks, it doesn't get much better than that.

The recipe I'm sharing from Tommy's Country Ham House is the stellar house-blended country chicken sausage. The recipe wasn't hard to acquire—the guy is just so nice. If I'm unable to return to Tommy's Country Ham House, I will certainly give this easy-to-follow recipe a shot in my home kitchen. And maybe if I'm lucky, some of Tommy's genuine persistence mixed with ability and creativity will rub off on me.

3 tablespoons canola oil, divided

1 large yellow onion, minced

1 pound ground chicken

⅓ cup finely shredded fresh sage

¾ teaspoon kosher salt

¾ teaspoon freshly cracked black pepper

Pinch of cayenne pepper

COUNTRY CHICKEN SAUSAGE

Heat 2 tablespoons of the oil in a medium skillet over medium-high heat. Add the onion and sauté until soft and translucent, 6 to 8 minutes.

In a large bowl combine the onions with the chicken, sage, salt, pepper, and cayenne. Using your hands, form the mixture into patties, about 1-inch thick and 3 inches in diameter. Refrigerate until ready to cook.

Preheat the oven to 350 degrees. Place a skillet over medium-low heat and add the remaining 1 tablespoon oil. Brown the sausages in two batches for about 2 minutes per side. Place on a baking sheet and bake for 8 minutes, or until fully cooked.

Serves 6 to 8.

Wade's Restaurant

Spartanburg, South Carolina

The words *interesting, hardworking,* and *sharp* come to mind when I think about Wade Lindsey. Wade is the proprietor and entrepreneur behind the popular small-town eatery Wade's Restaurant in Spartanburg. The community has embraced and followed Wade's mantra, "Eat at Wade's." They are just doing as they have been told. Wade is a country boy who found his way to Spartanburg by hitchhiking. It was a one-way trip, and once Wade was enrolled in school and busy falling in love with wife, Betty, the Spartanburg chapter of his life was well underway. He was seeking new adventures and making a place for himself and a new family. In the 1940s, Spartanburg was a town full of factories. After several years of working at a looming factory, Wade determined he would take charge of his own future and saw opportunity sandwiched between his factory and the factory next door. In 1947, the year a loaf of bread sold for thirteen cents, Wade Lindsey purchased an old grocery store wedged between the two largest factories in Spartanburg and started his restaurant.

The guy wasn't a chef or restaurateur, but with thousands of factory workers on either side of his new business, he knew there was a serious need for a place that served a hot lunch. With a little creativity, sliced bread, and hotdogs, he opened the doors to his future. With a growing demand for both in-restaurant dining and catering services, Wade's grew beyond his family's wildest dreams. But then the factories left town, just as they did in much of America, in search of cheaper overseas labor. Wade's business needed to shift with the changing economy. He turned his focus toward feeding families and the community, reaching a larger percentage of Spartanburg residents. A meat and three–style restaurant was born, and it was a hit. By this time, Wade's had graduated from its original wooden shack and was now a large cinder-block building that could accommodate hundreds of hungry customers.

As in most restaurant families, Wade and Betty's children were raised in the business and fell in love with the operations. They learned the ins and outs and started picking up where Wade left off. Sadly, in 1997 Wade Lindsey passed away four months after the restaurant's fiftieth anniversary. He was 87 years old.

The business model and the culture that Wade created lasted against all odds. Wade and Betty's children and grandchildren operate the restaurant today, continuing to nurture the culture, sense of belonging, credibility, quality, and consistency that Wade built over the decades.

As I read over the menu at Wade's, I admired how the staff has taken old favorites and recreated them to make them relevant and new. Adapting well to changing tastes, Wade's focuses on healthy ingredients and local produce, while still respecting what got them to meat and three hall of fame status. When I asked for Wade's turkey and dressing recipe, the response was a chuckle. I knew immediately I'd be forced to recreate this favorite, but I completely understood why I'd never get my hands on the original recipe. I know my turkey and dressing is tasty, but at Wade's it's taken sixty years, multiple generations, and a serious passion for food and service to perfect what's being dished up daily. Enjoy this version and know it's close to Wade's dressing. But don't take my word for it. Pack a bag, go to Spartanburg, and try the original for yourself.

TURKEY DRESSING

Combine the turkey meats, cornbread, white bread, celery, and onions in a large bowl. Fold together well. Add the poultry seasoning, sage, salt, butter, broth, and beaten eggs. Stir gently until well mixed. Grease a 9 x 13-inch baking dish with the chilled butter. Pour the dressing into the pan and refrigerate for 30 minutes.

Preheat the oven to 350 degrees. Cover the pan with aluminum foil and bake the dressing for 30 minutes. Remove the foil and increase the oven temperature to 400 degrees. Bake for about 10 minutes, until the top is browned. Let the dressing stand for 15 minutes before serving.

Serves 10 to 12.

2 cups chopped, cooked dark turkey meat

1 cup chopped, cooked white turkey meat

5 cups crumbled cornbread

3 cups cubed white bread

2 cups chopped celery

3 cups chopped onions

2 tablespoons poultry seasoning

1 teaspoon dried sage

2 teaspoons salt

1 cup (2 sticks) butter, melted

4 cups chicken broth

3 eggs, beaten

Chilled butter for greasing pan

Downtown Café

Piedmont, South Carolina

The folks at Downtown Café in Piedmont serve a ton of breakfast and lunch plates in a short amount of time, from six in the morning until two in the afternoon, all with a Southern flair and love of regional staples. It may be a small family-run restaurant in a small town, but there is nothing small about the flavors coming out of the tiny kitchen. The town of Piedmont is fortunate to have such a great restaurant. The community of five thousand residents is amazingly beautiful and boasts a surprisingly low unemployment rate and cost of living. That savings equals more money for the people of Piedmont to spend at the Downtown Café.

The Downtown Café appears to be your typical, humble meat and three restaurant offering breakfast and lunch, but when you taste the delicious food being served, you will understand how the café exceeds expectations with quality and consistency on each visit for every guest. This mom-and-pop restaurant delivers standard Southern meat and three staples with a few subtle twists and turns worth ordering. I played my way through the menu, looking for a gem, and when I overheard the staff hollering back and forth through the dining room for orders of the fresh field peas, I knew I had found the menu hook I was craving.

Coming up in the ranks of a variety of different kitchens, I learned one consistent lesson: keep the food simple and uncomplicated and allow the ingredient to shine. This recipe is a great example of this important lesson and can easily be recreated at home.

BUTTER FIELD PEAS

Place the peas in a colander and rinse with cold water to remove any debris. Fill a large pot with the water and bring to a boil over high heat. Add 2 tablespoons of the salt and the peas. Reduce the heat to medium-low and simmer the peas until tender but still slightly firm, 3 to 5 minutes. Drain the peas in a colander.

In a cast-iron skillet or sauté pan, melt the butter. Add the onions and cook until translucent, about 10 minutes. Add peas and cook, stirring, for 5 to 7 minutes. Just before removing from the heat season with salt and pepper to taste. Stir in the basil and lemon peel, if using.

Serves 8.

NOTE: You can use any variety of fresh field peas in the recipe: Big Red Ripper, Bird, Colossus, Cow, Crowder, Hercules, Iron Clay, Mississippi Silver, Old Timer, Pinkeye, Polecat, Purple Hull, Rattlesnake, Rucker, Shanty, Stick Up, Turkey Craw, Wash Day, Whippoorwill, or Zipper.

2 pounds fresh seasonal field peas

1 gallon water

2 ½ tablespoons kosher salt, divided

2 tablespoons butter

½ cup finely chopped yellow onion

Freshly cracked black pepper

1 teaspoon chopped fresh basil leaves

1 teaspoon finely grated lemon peel, optional

TENNESSEE

The Tennessee state seal tells the whole story of the state, with the symbols of agriculture and commerce full-center. In the early days, the riverways in the delta helped build the state's value as a center of commerce and distribution. Now, with the home office of FedEx in Memphis, that tradition continues on a worldwide scale. With about 50 percent of the state made up of farmland, Tennessee is serious about the farm-to-table movement. The funny thing is, for Tennesseans, it isn't a movement. Instead, it's just the way they've provided for and fed their families and neighbors for hundreds of years. Hard work yields good crops, while the friendly vibes from the Memphis Delta to the mountains of East Tennessee create the perfect recipe for good food and good times. And whatever you do in Tennessee, don't forget the music.

The landscape of Tennessee includes a varied degree of landscapes, from the bluff city of Memphis to the foothills in the East. In the southwest corner of the state, you'll find the delta with its heavy focus on barbecue, the blues, and its status as the "birthplace of rock and roll." The "King" still has not left the building here, if you catch my drift. In the middle of the state, you'll find the epicenter of the country music universe, Nashville. The streets downtown are lined with stores selling cowboy boots and ten gallon hats, and the air is filled with the twang of guitars. In the mountains of East Tennessee, you run into the bluegrass crowd, a music style that has actually regained popularity in the past few years. Originating with early Scottish, Irish, and English immigrants, "mountain music" has a very distinct and individual sound altogether.

Although their taste in music may differ, Tennesseans agree on one important thing—good, home-cooked Southern food. This state has so many meat and three restaurants that my decision on which restaurants to visit was difficult. On the flip side, I knew that no matter where I ended up, I would be well taken care of. The places I found and the people I met didn't disappoint. For Tennessee, the meat and three restaurant is a time-honored tradition and a natural gathering place.

Tennessee is known as the Volunteer State because of its residents' eagerness to take part in the War of 1812. Despite this fact and the warm hospitality I encountered during my travels, there were still some stubborn holdouts who wouldn't part with their precious family recipes. Oh well, that just brings me more adventure and challenge in recreating the delicious food I ate there.

Aretha Frankenstein's

Chattanooga, Tennessee

'm sliding Aretha Frankenstein's in Chattanooga into the mix because the food is outrageous, consistent, and delicious, the staff is genuine, and the concept is killer. It doesn't serve fast food; it offers homemade food with attitude. It's had a huge impact on the small, family-owned dining scene in Chattanooga. Aretha Frankenstein's is banging out some serious dishes. If you find yourself waiting on a Saturday or Sunday, you'd better pack a snack to tide you over because the word is out, and the line forms around the corner.

Breakfast lovers beware because the restaurant boasts a huge breakfast menu. From the pancakes, to the waffles, to the coffee drinks, to the egg combinations, there are limitless options. With my focus on breakfast at the restaurant, I know you are asking why this restaurant made my list of the best of family-operated meat and three restaurants. It's because the folks at Aretha Frankenstein's don't stop at breakfast. They are open from sunup to midnight with a menu that is full of eclectic, original, and traditional combinations.

I tried breakfast, I sampled lunch, and then came back for dinner. I had a hard time keeping track of all my meals, but the best thing I found on the menu was the perfectly executed buttermilk biscuits. And I do mean perfectly— like, where did these people come from? Even though biscuits seem to be such a simple thing, I see more biscuit failures than any other offering.

Here is the deal with biscuits: they're kind of a love thing. They require patience and lots of understanding of the yummy little things happening with your ingredients. Be gentle. Don't rush. Pour yourself a large glass of sweet tea, take a deep breath, and understand that the time you invest in your biscuits will be returned to your tummy tenfold. If you overwork the dough, knead it too hard, or even use off-temperature butter, they will be dense and not flaky. Biscuit dough is delicate in its consistency, and the fragileness of the dough reminds me of a hybrid mix of cake batter and pie crust. Like pie dough, biscuit dough must have a perfectly measured mixture of flour and cold fat, with the butter getting cut into the flour. And, similar to cake batter, there has to be a leavening agent—baking powder. Then you add the wet ingredients. Most commonly used in the South is buttermilk, although there are recipes that call for milk or even water. This addition of the wet ingredient creates a very wet, sticky dough. This is where most inexperienced biscuit makers are thrown a curve ball and begin to add tons of flour to compensate for the wetness of the dough. Stop! Put flour on your working surface, pour the wet mixture out and gently tap the dough flat. Cut, flip, but don't press. These are the secrets of real biscuit making that Aretha Frankenstein's executes so well. Seems simple, right? Try it a few times, though, before you start bragging. And when you visit Aretha Frankenstein's, after you book your table, be sure to thank the folks for sharing the original recipe.

BUTTERMILK BISCUITS

3 cups all-purpose flour

2 teaspoons salt

2 ½ tablespoons sugar, plus more for sprinkling

2 ½ tablespoons baking powder

½ cup (1 stick) butter, cut into small pieces

1 ⅓ cups buttermilk

Preheat the oven to 350 degrees.

Mix the flour, salt, sugar, and baking powder in a large bowl. Add the butter and cut it into the flour mixture, using a pastry blender or two knives, until the butter pieces are the size of peas. Pour the buttermilk into the flour mixture and continue mixing until all the flour is incorporated. The dough will be wet and sticky.

Place the dough on a floured board and gently fold the dough to make sure it is thoroughly mixed. Pat the dough into a circle about 1 inch high. Use a Mason jar with a 3-inch diameter mouth or 3-inch biscuit cutter to cut biscuits. Place the biscuits with their sides touching in a cast-iron skillet or on baking sheet. Sprinkle with a little sugar. Bake for 20 minutes, or until the tops and bottoms are golden brown.

Serves 6 to 8.

Chandler's Deli

Knoxville, Tennessee

My theory about meat and three restaurants is that the locations of these comfort food destinations are in the most unlikely places. This theory again proves true for Chandler's Deli in Knoxville. The restaurant has set up shop in a former Taco Bell building. If you're lucky enough to make the trip and belly up to the bar, keep these pointers in mind: show up hungry and leave with leftovers.

Charles and Gwen Chandler just wanted a good home-cooking, family-owned restaurant that served Southern staples. Since their community didn't seem to have what they were looking for, they decided to take on the mission themselves. The concept came together easily as they started with a short list of perfectly cooked offerings. As time went on and customer demand increased, they added a few tasty additions, and their simple menu blossomed into a list that has Knoxville locals and visitors alike clamoring for more. The menu at Chandler's may appear ambitious at first, offering a variety of Southern staples including barbecued ribs, fried fish, fried chicken dinner, black-eyed peas any way you want to eat them, and collards that will convert you to a Southerner. Once you taste their offerings, though, you will see that the menu is not ambitious—it's just confident. For me, the sweet potato pie was so perfectly done that it won my heart and my stomach.

When I started my journey through ten states to research the best meat and three restaurants, I had a preconceived notion about how each of the Southern eateries I visited would gladly offer up their recipes to me. I was dead wrong. Usually the recipes I want the most are the ones the restaurants seem least likely to share. They guard their family recipes with an admirable, although somewhat frustrating, devotion. I might say, "I'd love to share your sweet potato pie recipe," and they offer creamed corn, or I ask for a barbecue recipe, and I'm delivered field peas. The owners are slick, crafty, and seemingly one step ahead of me and my requests to find the best original recipes.

I'm giving sweet potato pie a shot on my own, though, and know a few tricks that turn the humble tuberous root into a rock star pie that you can add to your cooking repertoire. But if you get a chance, visit Chandler's Deli and try the original.

SWEET POTATO PIE

Piecrust

1 ½ cups all-purpose flour

3 tablespoons sugar

¼ teaspoon salt

½ cup (1 stick) cold butter, cut into ½-inch cubes

1 teaspoon grapeseed oil

¼ cup ice water

Filling

5 medium sweet potatoes

3 large eggs

¾ cup heavy cream

¼ cup white sugar

⅓ cup packed brown sugar

1 ½ teaspoons butter, melted

¼ teaspoon salt

½ teaspoon ground cinnamon

½ teaspoon ground mace

½ teaspoon vanilla extract

For the piecrust, place the flour, sugar, and salt in the bowl of a food processor and pulse to blend. Add the butter and oil and pulse until the butter pieces are the size of small peas. Add half of the ice water and pulse to blend. Continuing adding ice water, 1 tablespoon at a time, pulsing after each addition, until the mixture barely begins to hold together. Place a large piece of plastic wrap on the counter. Dump the pie dough onto the wrap and gather the dough into a mound. Wrap securely and refrigerate for 1 hour or up to 1 day.

Remove the pie dough from the refrigerator and unwrap. Place the dough on a lightly floured surface and roll it into a 13-inch circle, about ⅛-inch thick. Lift the dough and place it in a 9-inch pie pan. Trim the edges evenly, leaving about 1 inch overhang. Fold the edges under and crimp. Place the pie pan in the freezer for 30 minutes.

Preheat the oven to 350 degrees.

Place a sheet of parchment paper over the piecrust and fill it with pie weights. Bake the piecrust for 20 minutes. Remove from the oven and lift out the parchment paper and weights. Prick the bottom of the crust with a fork in several places. Return the crust to the oven and bake for an additional 10 minutes. Let cool completely before adding the filling.

Increase the oven temperature to 400 degrees.

For the filling, place the sweet potatoes on a baking sheet and bake them about 1 hour, until tender. Set aside until cool enough to handle.

Reduce the oven temperature to 325 degrees

Cut the potatoes into halves lengthwise and scoop out the flesh. Place it in the bowl of a food processor and pulse until creamy and smooth.

Beat the eggs with a hand mixer until frothy. Add 3 cups of the pureed sweet potatoes, the heavy cream, white sugar, brown sugar, butter, salt, cinnamon, mace, and vanilla. Mix until well blended and smooth. Pour the mixture into the cooled piecrust. Bake the pie on the middle rack of the oven for 30 minutes, turn the pie 180 degrees, and continue baking until the center is set and the edges start to rise, about 15 more minutes. The filling should be firm and the edges may be slightly puffed.

Serves 10.

City Café East

Nashville, Tennessee

The love of incredible food and family run as deep as the Mississippi River in the South. For Chef George Reed and his wife, Amy, the connection to food and guests is incredibly strong. The City Café East in Nashville has the cozy charm of a living room, and the food reminds me of Grandma's, if she were a professional cook for thirty years, that is. Chef George has the knowledge, the recipes, and the love to make his Southern-inspired meat and three a Nashville favorite.

His barbecued brisket is a thing of beauty. I usually avoid conversations about barbecue because they often turn into debates that consumers base on personal taste and pit masters base on technique. I'm not an authority on either. Chef George was pushed into offering his barbecue at the City Café after a single day's offering of his brisket as a daily special became a demand that was beyond control. Recognizing a hit when he saw it, George knew a special day dedicated to the brisket would satisfy all the hungry customers and move his restaurant one step closer to becoming an institution.

When I let him know that I wanted to not only eat his barbecued brisket but also to share the recipe, I encountered a less agreeable version of Chef George. He was very protective of this brisket recipe, knowing full well that its secrets are keys to his success at the City Café East. With my limited barbecue experience, I was in for a real challenge in my attempt to replicate the City Café brisket and get the seal of approval from the man himself. Here is my version, and if I do say so myself, it's a solid attempt at a very difficult recipe. For the home cook, this recipe is an easy slam dunk and still uber delicious. Chef George was all smiles to see this come together, and I got his nod of approval; however, in my book the only true Nashville brisket is at City Café East. Be sure to come early because the line stays long all day. You may want to order two plates so you don't have to wait in line all over again.

BARBECUED BRISKET

1 (1-ounce) packet dry onion soup mix

2 tablespoons all-purpose flour

2 cloves garlic, crushed

1 large oven roasting bag

1 (6- to 7-pound) beef brisket, untrimmed

2 teaspoons salt

2 teaspoons freshly cracked black pepper

12 ounces beef broth

3 tablespoons Worcestershire sauce

Preheat the oven to 300 degrees.

Combine soup mix, flour, and garlic in the oven roasting bag. Close bag and shake well.

Season brisket with the salt and pepper and place in bag. Pour in the beef broth and Worcestershire sauce. Close the bag and place in a shallow baking pan. With a sharp knife cut a few slits in the top of the bag to vent it. Place in the oven and bake for 3 ½ hours, or until tender.

Serves 12 to 14.

The Copper Kettle

Nashville, Tennessee

Many years ago I was introduced to the tasty meat and three menu from Nashville's Copper Kettle during a television shoot that they catered. So, for many days consecutively, I ate the food from the Copper Kettle, met the people, and became friends with them. Now, flash forward to my research for this book as I'm searching for my favorite meat and three restaurants all over the state of Tennessee. I stumble again upon the Copper Kettle.

My rediscovery of the Copper Kettle quickly reminded me that I wasn't roughing it when I was on this long and grueling television shoot in Nashville. In fact, I was well taken care of. The television industry term for on-set catered meals is "craft services," and this moniker did absolutely no justice to the quality of the food whatsoever. It wasn't "crafty"; it was spectacular and memorable. My recent visit was incognito. I wanted to slide in, eat, and slide out so as not to be noticed. Honestly, the food was even better than I remembered—real Southern food in a meat and three setting. The entrées were familiar, but better, and the flavors were more developed than I encountered years before. I took notice of the delicate vegetable preparation; they actually tasted like vegetables. Each one had its own identity and flavor. The beans and corn tasted the way you might imagine them from a farmers' market, still firm to the tooth but cooked and well-seasoned. This respectful treatment of the often overlooked side dishes seemed to me more of an accomplishment than insane fried chicken or a bottomless pit of meatloaf. What I encountered was awesome. The vegetable department at some meat and three restaurants can be lacking. I mean, I'm all for thoroughly cooking green beans, but not for twelve hours. At the Copper Kettle my entire meal was over the top, but I chose veggies as the star of the meal. Check out the Copper Kettle in Nashville to make some delicious food memories and enjoy the staff's attention to detail and the skill in preparing authentic Southern food.

GLAZED CARROTS

2 pounds large carrots

½ cup (1 stick) butter, divided

1 cup packed light brown sugar, divided

½ tablespoon kosher salt

Freshly cracked black pepper

1 teaspoon nutmeg

Bring a large pot of salted water to a full boil. Fill a large bowl with 4 cups of ice and cover with water.

Peel the carrots and cut into ½-inch-thick rounds. Add the carrots to the boiling water and cook for 4 minutes at a full boil. Drain the carrots and place them in the ice water to stop the cooking. Remove the carrots from the ice bath and pat dry.

Heat a large skillet over medium heat. Add ¼ cup of the butter and ½ cup of the brown sugar. Add the carrots to the butter mixture. Cook, stirring, for 2 to 3 minutes. Add the remaining ½ cup sugar and remaining ¼ cup butter and stir until the vegetables are evenly coated. Add the salt, pepper, and nutmeg. Serve immediately with the pan sauce.

Serves 8 to 10.

DeJAVU

Memphis, Tennessee

DeJAVU Restaurant in Memphis is a one-of-a-kind embodiment of awesome. My first impression of the restaurant was on a 110-degree day when Chef Gary Williams welcomed me into his restaurant just as you would invite someone into your home. Not only is the chef and restaurateur a fabulous cook, he drives the business and carries the name with consistency, credibility, and Southern charm. Chef Gary is a transplant from New Orleans who came to Memphis after Hurricane Katrina. He arrived in the Bluff City with only a few possessions but armed with years of practical cooking as a professional chef. That experience led him to build a restaurant empire called DeJAVU. Chef Gary and crew are known in the neighborhood for authentic New Orleans dishes, but even more so for the superb vegetarian offerings that make up most of his eclectic Southern-inspired menu. From pasta dishes and sides, to seafood, to the traditional New Orleans jambalaya, the cuisine at DeJAVU has swept up from the Gulf of Mexico and settled into Memphis.

Chef Gary was more than accommodating when I requested his recipes and offered several that I've kept to myself. For this book, however, I wanted to recreate a popular dish from the restaurant and see if Chef Gary would give me his approval. I gravitated to barbecued shrimp, a dish that I've often featured on menus of my own. Although my recipe has always been tasty, the barbecued shrimp at DeJAVU seems to have a special voodoo that captures more than taste. The familiar flavors are deep and well developed, but the dish feels light, more like a snack. At DeJAVU Chef Gary offers up these yummy little guys as a side or an entrée. Here is the suggestion of the day: grab a change of clothes, top off the tank in the car, and call ahead to DeJAVU in Memphis. There are limited tables and a long line of hungry locals waiting for more of Chef Gary's well-seasoned Creole magic. Tell him I sent you, and "let the good times roll."

16 jumbo shrimp, heads on and unpeeled

½ cup Worcestershire sauce

2 tablespoons fresh lemon juice

1 teaspoon freshly cracked black pepper

3 teaspoons Creole seasoning

2 teaspoons minced garlic

1 cup cold butter, cut into small pieces

French bread

BARBECUED SHRIMP

Heat a large skillet over medium-high. Add the shrimp, Worcestershire sauce, lemon juice, black pepper, Creole seasoning, and garlic. Cook, stirring often, until the shrimp turn slightly pink, about 90 seconds on each side. Reduce the heat to medium-low and stir in the butter, a few pieces at a time, until all the butter is melted and incorporated. Remove the skillet from the heat. Place the shrimp in a bowl and pour the pan sauce over the shrimp. Serve with French bread for dipping.

Serves 2.

Kleer-Vu Lunchroom

Murfreesboro, Tennessee

The Kleer-Vu Lunchroom in Murfreesboro serves the masses from a tiny little steam table in a tiny little building, but the food is as big and as stellar as the restaurant's reputation in the community. Customer satisfaction, if you ask any restaurant operator, is essential for sustainability and success in business. With the changing food climate in Nashville and surrounding cities, you would assume the small mom-and-pop operations may take a hit. But nothing is altered, nothing is changing, and the lines just continue to get longer at this local favorite.

People often say not to judge a book by its cover, and I believe this rule couldn't be truer for the Kleer-Vu Lunchroom. The exterior has little to offer aesthetically other than protection from the elements, and the dining room has similar qualities—you'll find only a place to rest your butt and a table for your plate. But what it lacks in ambiance, the Kleer-Vu makes up for with a heaping dose of amazing Southern food and a welcome mat that stretches all the way to Music City. The customers who support the tiny little meat and three are like family. Some are new, but most are regulars. The regulars have had children, and their children have also had children. The Kleer-Vu Lunchroom that has fed generations of folks in Murfreesboro for years just continues to expand.

I tried chess pie, chocolate pie, fried chicken, mac 'n' cheese, greens, and cornbread, and I think I drank two gallons of sweet tea. My favorite on this visit was the classic and humble Southern chess pie. Chess pie may seem to be a strange dessert if you're from north of the Mason-Dixon Line, but I'm pretty certain this gooey confection is a gift from the Gods. Despite the sweetness of my selection, in normal fashion, the Southern hospitality was immediately turned off when I asked for the guarded family recipe. Surprised? No, I think not. Challenged for approval and, ultimately, the ability to eat chess pie in my own kitchen? Yes, absolutely. So here's my recreation.

4 eggs

2 ½ cups sugar

½ cup whole milk

6 tablespoons butter

1 tablespoon cornmeal

2 tablespoons all-purpose
flour

Finely grated peel and
juice of 1 lemon

Pinch of kosher salt

1 unbaked piecrust

SOUTHERN CHESS PIE

Preheat the oven to 425 degrees.

Mix together the eggs, sugar, milk, butter, cornmeal, flour, lemon peel and juice, and salt in a large bowl. Stir until the sugar dissolves. Pour filling into the piecrust. Bake for 12 minutes. Reduce the oven temperature to 325 degrees and bake 25 to 30 minutes longer, until the pie filling is set. Remove and let cool. Slice into wedges when cool and serve at room temperature.

Serves 8.

Rose Garden Restaurant

Silver Point, Tennessee

From the moment you arrive at the Rose Garden Restaurant in Silver Point, there is no doubt you are smack in the middle of the small-town South and headed for some good eats. The building, located slightly behind the only gas station in town, is nothing special. When you walk in the door, you are greeted by a sign that pretty much says it all: "Welcome to the Rose Garden. We prepare each plate to order.... We are not a fast food restaurant. Please be patient. Thank you." In other words, sit down, relax, and your food will come when it's ready. The dining room is a small, open room where customers often greet one another by yelling across the room as you would in your own home at a family gathering. The waitresses are friendly and quick on their feet, even if none of them is under thirty-five. They wear blue aprons with their names embroidered on them.

The meats and veggies of the day are handwritten on dry-erase boards, and the waitresses love to brag about the homemade pies. They also remind you that if you happen to be in town on Saturday, that's spaghetti night, and possibly the biggest thing going on in this quaint little town.

As I perused the menu, I saw a plethora of traditional Southern favorites. One thing that never ceases to amaze me about Southerners is their ability to take something innocent and healthy, like a vegetable, and turn it into a fattening, decadent treat. The Rose Garden Restaurant was no different in this respect, with several fried vegetable options to choose from including okra, green beans, squash, and green tomatoes. I went for the grand poobah of Southern fried veggies, the fried green tomatoes. I wasn't disappointed and was happy to "be patient" until they arrived. The cornmeal crust on the outside of the slightly tart tomatoes was nice and crispy, but not overcooked, and the tomatoes themselves were warm with a delicious mix of sweet and sour you can't find anywhere else. I devoured every last one and was happy to pay whatever price was asked of me at the candy and gum counter where the register was located.

If you've never had the pleasure of enjoying a nice, hot fried green tomato, here's your chance. Enjoy the following recipe for a true taste of the South, and if you're ever passing through Silver Point, be sure to stop by the Rose Garden Restaurant, as long as you're not in a hurry.

½ cup yellow cornmeal

½ teaspoon garlic powder

½ teaspoon onion powder

1 cup all-purpose flour

2 large whole eggs, beaten

6 green tomatoes, sliced
½-inch thick

1 cup vegetable oil

Kosher salt to taste

FRIED GREEN TOMATOES

Mix the cornmeal, garlic powder, and onion powder in a small bowl. In two separate bowls place the flour and eggs. Dredge the tomatoes in the flour mixture, then in the eggs, and finally in the cornmeal mixture, pressing gently to help the breading adhere.

Heat the oil in a large, deep skillet over high heat. Working in small batches, cook the tomatoes until golden brown, about 2 minutes per side. Transfer the cooked tomatoes to a paper towel–lined baking sheet to drain. Season with salt while the tomatoes are still warm.

Serves 8.

Southern Star

Chattanooga, Tennessee

The Southern Star in Chattanooga offers simple, fresh, authentic Southern cuisine and the Southern hospitality to match. It fits perfectly into the meat and three mold, but delivers its offerings with style and well-thought combinations. Most Southern meat and three restaurants are respectful to the original version of their replicated dishes, but somehow at the Southern Star the food feels less reinvented and more creative. Owners Rick and Nancy Adams have created the environment and the appropriately balanced menu to appeal to anyone, whether they are a fan of Southern food or not. They offer tasty options including the poppy seed chicken and Brunswick stew that blew me away. Just as my feet began to leave the ground from flavor euphoria, the banana pudding and lemon bars kept me grounded by reminding me of something familiar and yet uniquely delicious.

I enjoy Chattanooga. The culture, history, and landscape of this interesting little big town make for a fun trip. Over the past few years the food scene has blossomed. Restaurants are popping up everywhere from Signal Mountain to downtown, all serving great food. The Southern Star fits in perfectly with the landscape of Chattanooga and has the quality to stick around.

Choosing a dish to represent the Southern Star wasn't as clear and easy as some of my other choices for restaurants I visited. I wanted to offer a little of the creative spirit I encountered here. I decided on baked grits for a few reasons. One, they are delicious. Two, they are made with a tangy sharp Cheddar cheese. Three, they are baked, creating a texture that's slightly different from the creamy mound of grits you find at most Southern-style restaurants. Although I was getting used to rejection, I again asked for the original recipe, and not surprisingly, they denied my request. But I've recreated it and am happy with the results. Baked grits are easy to make at home, but think about planning a trip to Chattanooga to taste what's happening at the Southern Star.

5 cups water

2 teaspoons kosher salt, plus more to taste

1 ½ cups grits

2 cups grated sharp white Cheddar cheese, divided

2 tablespoons whole-wheat flour

1 teaspoon chopped fresh basil

1 teaspoon chopped fresh thyme

Freshly cracked black pepper

2 cloves garlic

3 large eggs

½ cup heavy cream

SHARP CHEDDAR BAKED GRITS

Preheat the oven to 350 degrees.

Pour the water and salt in a saucepan and bring to a full boil over medium-high heat. Slowly add the grits to the water, whisking constantly. Reduce the heat to medium and simmer, whisking occasionally, until thickened, 15 to 20 minutes.

In a large bowl combine 1 cup of cheese, the flour, basil, thyme, and pepper. In a small bowl, mash the garlic with a generous pinch of salt, pressing with a fork until the mixture forms a paste. Whisk the mashed garlic and the cheese mixture into the grits until well incorporated. Taste and add salt and pepper as needed. Remove from the heat and let cool slightly

In a medium bowl beat the eggs and cream with a pinch of salt. Stir the egg mixture into the grits and fold together. Pour the grits into a 9 x 13-inch glass or ceramic baking dish. Sprinkle the remaining cheese evenly over the top of the grits. Bake about 1 hour, until puffed and browned on top.

Serves 8.

The Cupboard Restaurant

Memphis, Tennessee

I have an opinion about the Cupboard Restaurant in Memphis. I believe that this may be the meat and three restaurant that others of this style sample from and take note of. Just a theory. This place is a machine that from daybreak to sundown has fed generations for more than seventy years. The restaurant still does it as perfectly as it did when it served its first plate in 1943.

When The Cupboard first opened its doors, Memphis was experiencing a time in the national spotlight. The famous Memphis Belle B-17 airplane neared the last of twenty-five bombing missions over Germany without a single crew causality. Beale Street was home to African American musicians, who brought the cotton field hollers into all the amazing new juke joints and clubs. Just a few blocks from Beale Street, WDIA was the first radio station in the United States that had an all-African American format and African American disc jockeys. Legendary blues man B.B. King was a DJ on the historic station and began recording at Sun Studio later in the 1950s as his career

developed. Memphis during this time spawned incredible national businesses, including the country's first self-service grocery, Piggly Wiggly, and Kemmons Wilson's Holiday Inn.

In 1992 Charles Cavallo purchased The Cupboard and continued serving Southern food and catering his delicious plate meals to hungry locals and visitors. The story behind the business is as strong as the family behind the counter. These folks have always focused on quality and served as the epitome of Southern hospitality. The restaurant moved to a new location, on Union Avenue, in 2000, a setting that is far larger and likely more efficient in feeding the hundreds of daily customers.

Despite its many tasty offerings, I decided to feature The Cupboard's simple carrot-raisin salad. My memories of the Southern concoction date back to my childhood when a great-great-aunt, who smelled funny, always brought the dish to family gatherings such as funerals and reunions. The Cupboard's version is so tasty that it will wipe away any negative memories you have of this iconic chilled Southern side.

CARROT-RAISIN SALAD

Finely shred the carrots into a large bowl. Add the yogurt, raisins, pineapple, lemon juice, and honey and stir well. Taste and season as needed with salt and pepper. Refrigerate for 20 minutes and serve chilled.

Serves 12.

1 pound carrots

8 ounces plain yogurt

½ cup raisins

1 cup canned pineapple, minced

2 tablespoons lemon juice

1 tablespoon honey

Salt and pepper to taste

Wally's Restaurant

Chattanooga, Tennessee

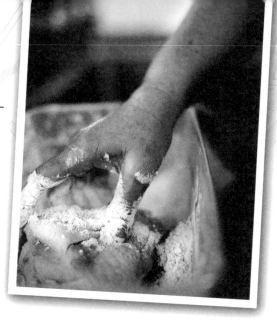

I n 1937 Wally Alexander opened his eponymous restaurant, Wally's, in Chattanooga. Although he had little experience in the restaurant industry, Wally saw a need in the small but growing community. When I think about the restaurant's early days, I imagine the music of Glenn Miller and his orchestra singing Chattanooga Choo Choo playing in the background, barely audible over the sound of roller skates worn by the original carhop waitstaff. Wally identified his market as a young crowd with growing families who needed good, fresh, but fast food. Now flash forward nearly eight decades. The food landscape of Chattanooga has changed, and Wally's may be slightly different from what it was in its infancy, but its principles, food quality, and overall love for the community is still priority number one.

Fried chicken in the South is a big deal, but Wally's introduced a delicious method for near guiltless pleasure, the breaded chicken tender. The flavor and texture is reminiscent of Southern fried chicken but with less of an assault on your thighs and waistband. I can eat Wally's chicken tenders by the dozen, which I'm pretty sure completely negates what I just said. They are light, fluffy, and crunchy with just enough saltiness and sweetness so you can't stop eating them. It's the house specialty and for good reason. Chicken tenders are easily my favorite of Wally's meat and three offerings. In the true spirit of Southern hospitality, Wally's was actually kind and generous enough to share the original recipe.

HAND-BREADED CHICKEN TENDERS

Season the chicken with salt, pepper, and garlic powder. Place the eggs in a bowl and beat. Combine the breadcrumbs and cheese in another bowl. Dredge the chicken in the egg mixture, then in the breadcrumb mixture.

Heat 3 tablespoons of the oil in a large, nonstick skillet over medium-high. Add half of chicken and cook until browned and cooked through, about 4 minutes on each side. Remove from pan. Repeat with the remaining 3 tablespoons oil and chicken. Serve immediately.

Serves 6.

2 pounds chicken tenders

1 teaspoon kosher salt

1 teaspoon freshly cracked black pepper

1 teaspoon garlic powder

3 large eggs

1 cup dry breadcrumbs

1 cup freshly grated Parmesan cheese

6 tablespoons canola oil, divided

Wendell Smith's Restaurant

Nashville, Tennessee

Wendell Smith's in Nashville is one of those down-home joints we refer to in the subtitle of this book. I just can't find another word to describe it better. The story of how it became what it is today is worth sharing. It starts like this: so a guy walks into a liquor store and says, "There should be a restaurant next door."

Jakie Cook was working as a clerk at Wendell Smith's (the liquor store) named for his father-in-law, when he had this brilliant epiphany. The restaurant was founded in 1952. Within a few years, Jakie was running the liquor store and the restaurant. His theory was spot on: have some eats and walk next door for a bottle on the way home. The retro exterior has been modified some over the past sixty years, but the menu and the family atmosphere haven't changed a bit. Now Jakie's son, Benji, is breaking into the business with huge shoes to fill, because the iconic restaurant has a reputation to uphold as Nashville's premier meat and three.

In classic form, the restaurant serves the best of the best each day. It's Christmas for a gastronome, with Mondays featuring beef-tips and noodles and Tuesdays, salmon patties and peas. It's almost too good to be true because the progression of the selections never fails to improve.

I'm going right for the jugular on this one.

The liver and onions are silly delicious and served on Thursday or, if you ask nicely, any day. The reason for this dish's popularity is Wendell Smith's recipe and the quality of the liver. So many restaurants with large menus forget the details within the details and leave out the obvious steps of creating huge flavor in each offering. This is not the case at Wendell Smith's. The restaurant grew over time, and as it grew, the staff perfected each and every detail so that no matter how busy the restaurant got, the quality stayed the same.

This brings us back to liver. If you have eaten liver and not enjoyed the dish, I know that it was because of the preparation. Stop for a second and remember, as I tell my children: try it thirteen times before you say you don't enjoy it. Wendell Smith's liver and onions is absolutely delicious. The liver is tender, not too earthy, and with just enough salt and acid to counteract the iron. I would never have imagined liver so delicately prepared. I've eaten liver half the quality of Wendell Smith's in a five-star restaurant. So, without hesitation, I admit that Wendell Smith's Restaurant has the best liver I've enjoyed for some time. Plan ahead, check the menu online, or possibly call ahead, because you will want to know what the restaurant is serving for the day, although no matter what day it is, you won't be disappointed.

COUNTRY PAN-FRIED LIVERS WITH CARAMELIZED ONIONS

1 pound beef liver

2 tablespoons butter

1 large onion, sliced

2 tablespoons sugar

1 cup all-purpose flour

2 teaspoons salt

Freshly cracked black pepper

1 cup oil for frying

Place the liver in a colander and drain, rinsing with cool water. Place on a baking sheet lined with paper towels to absorb moisture.

Place the butter in a large skillet over medium heat. Add the onions and cook until the onions begin to brown, about 10 minutes. Add the sugar and cook, stirring, until the onions caramelize, 15 to 20 minutes. Transfer the onions to a bowl and set aside to cool.

Place the flour in a shallow dish or bowl. Sprinkle the liver with the salt and black pepper. Dredge the liver in the flour, coating both sides. Shake off any excess.

Pour the oil into the pan and heat over medium-high. Add the liver and cook until browned on both sides, 3 to 4 minutes. Add the onions back to the pan and warm the entire dish for 30 seconds.

Serves 4.

TEXAS

Rodeos, cowboys, ten gallon hats, and the Alamo—these are just a few things that come to mind when you think of the state of Texas. Or even better might be: "Houston, we have a problem." The magnitude of the state often encourages people to refer to Texas as its own country. This giant in size and population has been under the governance of six different countries. But amid all that turmoil the people of Texas keep moving forward and developing their own distinct culture. Driving through the plains of Texas, I can understand how it has become the number one state in the nation for cattle production. The wide open plains almost make me want to slip on a pair of blue jeans and boots and saddle up. (I did say "almost.") I can't help but think of the movie *City Slickers* and be reminded that I would be the city guy.

Texas has a lot to offer even city folk like myself. With intriguing and artistic epicenters such as Austin, also known as the "Live Music Capital of the World," and metropolitan areas such as Dallas, which has more shopping centers per capita than any other city in the country, Texas is more than just wide-open plains and fields upon fields of cows and cowboys. If I'm looking to relax and unwind, I can just head on down to the Gulf Coast and soak in the beautiful seaside views in Corpus Christi. Or I can head on over to Houston and marvel at the mysteries of space travel. Texas has something to offer everyone.

Known for its oil production, Texas is an industrial giant. After the precious "black gold," however, Texas's second largest industry is agriculture, and it shows on the table. The meat and three restaurants that I was lucky enough to visit in this great state didn't disappoint. When they say everything is bigger in Texas, they definitely aren't leaving out the portion sizes at the local joints. And everywhere I went, I came across some amazing people with big smiles and even bigger hearts.

From the divine calling of Teresa Stephens at the Cast Iron Grill in Lubbock, to the commitment by the family running Babe's Chicken Dinner House in Roanoke, to the brotherly love found at Bryce's Cafeteria in Texarkana, everyone I came across had a real story and a genuine commitment to the customer's satisfaction. They welcome you like family and make sure you don't leave hungry. And no matter whose flag is flying overhead, Texans will be sure to keep their heads held high and their hospitality in the open.

AllGood Café

Dallas, Texas

One of the things I love about Southern meat and three restaurants is that the owners usually have a pretty good handle on where their food comes from. At the AllGood Café in Dallas, the restaurant workers not only know their suppliers, they make sure their customers do too by listing them on the front page of their menu. Their motto is straightforward: good food, good music, good times, good people. In other words, "it's all good."

The place itself is very welcoming with large windows that let in natural light, exposed brick pillars, and eclectic posters and historical items on every wall. Live music is offered Thursday through Sunday nights, and on the weekly craft night, customers can come and create something beautiful—maybe a homemade terrarium or a collection of coasters.

No matter what is on the calendar for entertainment, tasty food is always on the menu at the AllGood Café. On the day I wandered into town, the lunch menu grabbed my attention. I was looking for a little change from the usual meat and three fare, and I had stopped at the right place. AllGood's has a long list of tempting sandwiches, and although it was hard to steer myself away from my usual choice of a simple BLT, I finally settled on the Truck Stop Hot Beef.

The name alone was enough to grab my attention. When I think of truck stop food, I think of something that is going to stick to my ribs (and possibly my arteries) and get me through the long haul. This sandwich had it all: a mound of thinly sliced roast beef on deliciously grilled bread covered in a tasty gravy and melted cheese. The homemade mashed potatoes on the side were the perfect pairing. It felt like dinner but ate like lunch. The crispiness of the grilled sourdough bread perfectly balanced the roast beef slathered in the mushroom and onion gravy, and the melted cheese helped to meld it all together. It was definitely a lunch that would carry me through the long, grueling miles to my next stop. I imagined myself to be a road warrior who had been rejuvenated by roast beefy goodness.

I've done my best to capture the flavors and textures I was privileged enough to experience. The next time you're in Dallas, don't hesitate to wander into the AllGood Café, and just remember that no matter what you order, it's all good.

TRUCK STOP HOT BEEF SANDWICH

Preheat the oven to 325 degrees.

Remove buns from the package. Spread mustard-mayonnaise blend on the bottom of buns and top with cheese.

In a saucepan combine the gravy mix and water. Bring to a full boil over medium-high heat. Add the roast beef and, using a spoon, push it into the sauce until it is submerged.

Top the cheese with the meat and gravy and sprinkle with salt and pepper. Cover with the top halves of the buns and wrap each sandwich separately in aluminum foil.

Place the sandwiches on a baking sheet and bake for 20 to 25 minutes.

Serve the sandwiches in foil with a side of the gravy.

Serves 6.

NOTE: These sandwiches are better if refrigerated overnight and reheated before serving.

1 (8-count) package hamburger buns

½ cup mustard-mayonnaise blend

½ pound thinly sliced havarti cheese

1 (1-ounce) envelope au jus gravy mix

3 cups cold water

1 pound shaved deli roast beef, chopped

Salt and pepper to taste

Babe's Chicken Dinner House

Roanoke, Texas

Although most meat and three restaurants aren't part of a chain, Babe's Chicken Dinner House breaks the mold. It fits the criteria for the classic meat and three but has been so successful that it now boasts nine locations across the state. The original Babe's is housed in a 1908 warehouse that once housed a hardware store and then a grocery and plant shop before becoming a restaurant in 1993. The family-owned business is named for Mary Beth Vinyard—Babe was her nickname.

The building is as you would imagine a warehouse, a wide-open dining room with tall ceilings. Along the back wall is a large piece of stamped metal that used to be the ceiling of the old warehouse. Everyone who walks in is treated like family, and Paul Vinyard, a.k.a. Bubba, wants to make sure that everyone knows it, from the employees to the customers. Sadly, Babe passed away in 2008, but she left a legacy of delicious country food and the warm family atmosphere she helped to create.

Everything in this place is done with purpose. The location is a little off the beaten path, and there are no frivolities when it comes to the decor. At Babe's, the staff focuses on quality ingredients and delicious recipes. The owners aren't much for flashy advertising and still rely heavily on word of mouth, despite their growth. They still create their dishes in small batches, repeating the process as often as needed to make sure that every customer, from the first to the last, has the highest quality experience.

The fried chicken at Babe's is very tasty, just as you would expect at a joint called Babe's Chicken Dinner House. There is pride in the food, from the owner, to the cooks, to the server. After partaking in a very tasty and very filling dinner, I was ready to roll myself out the front door, but then the desserts caught my eye.

Pies in the South are a fixture at any holiday gathering, and taking a bite of pie always gives me the feeling of being surrounded by family—a welcome comfort to any road-weary traveler. Babe's gave me several options to choose from, and I was hard-pressed to pick a favorite, but I finally settled on the lemon meringue pie. There is something truly Southern about this concoction, and the marshmallowy meringue on top just beckons to you. The crust was deliciously flaky and buttery, and the filling had just enough sweetness and tartness to lull me into a full-on food coma.

I pulled out all the stops in trying to wrestle the recipe out of Bubba's hands but to no avail. I guess he wants to guard his success and make sure to preserve Babe's recipes and memory. I've recreated the recipe and hope that you'll have the same warm fuzzy feeling that Babe's pie gave me. If you happen to be traveling through the great state of Texas and you see a Babe's Chicken Dinner House, be sure to stop. You won't regret it. And make sure to save room for pie.

LEMON MERINGUE PIE

Preheat oven to 375 degrees.

For the filling, in a large bowl whisk the egg yolks.

Place the sugar, cornstarch, and salt in a saucepan. Add the water and milk and whisk until smooth. Bring to a boil over medium heat, whisking frequently as the mixture begins to thicken. Remove from the heat. Pour 1 cup of the hot milk mixture into the yolks and whisk until blended. Then pour the yolk mixture into the pan, whisking until blended. Add the lemon peel and juice. Bring to a simmer over medium-high heat and cook for 3 minutes. Remove from the heat and whisk in the butter until blended. Pour the mixture into the piecrust.

For the meringue, beat the egg whites with the cream of tartar and salt with a hand mixer on medium speed until soft peaks form. Increase speed to high and add the sugar, beating until the meringue just holds stiff, glossy peaks. Place a bit of the meringue between two fingers and rub to make sure the sugar has dissolved and is not gritty. Spread the meringue decoratively over the hot filling, covering the filling completely. Bake for 10 to 15 minutes, until meringue is golden brown. Let cool for 2 to 3 hours before slicing.

Serves 8.

Filling

6 egg yolks

1 ¼ cups sugar

¼ cup cornstarch

¼ teaspoon salt

1 ¼ cups water

¼ cup milk

2 tablespoons finely grated lemon peel

¼ cup fresh lemon juice

3 tablespoons butter

1 (9-inch) piecrust

Meringue

6 large egg whites

½ teaspoon cream of tartar

⅛ teaspoon salt

¾ cup white sugar

Black-Eyed Pea

Plano, Texas

You have to love a good comeback story and walking into the Black-Eyed Pea in Plano, I'm reminded that the restaurant business isn't much for second chances. Founded in 1975 in Oak Lawn, Texas, the Black-Eyed Pea restaurant quickly became a success with locations spreading across the South, mainly in Texas and Tennessee. In 2001, many of the restaurants closed in the midst of the economic downturn, but since that time and under new management, the chain has come back strong, providing country-casual dining.

As I walked into the restaurant in Plano, I took note of the wooden tables and booths and the light fixtures with, of course, a Southern Star on them. Since the restaurant is part of a larger business, there is a slightly more corporate feel to the dining room, but it's still very welcoming and inviting. As I perused the menu, I'm drawn to the chicken fried section.

Only in a Southern meat and three restaurant could you find a whole section of the menu devoted to chicken fried choices. For those of you who aren't from the South, "chicken fried" means pan-frying a cutlet of meat (chicken, pork, or steak) that has been dredged in seasoned flour. The "chicken" part of the dish suggests that the oil used to cook the meat has already been used to fry chicken. If you've never had it, I suggest a trip down South to try it out.

One of the best things about chicken fried dishes is that they come covered in delicious white gravy. Gravy, like biscuits, in the South is something of a treasure when it comes to family recipes. It's a frequent accoutrement to most meals although often overlooked and underappreciated. After a little debate, I decided on the chicken fried steak.

When my meal arrived, I couldn't help but devour every bite, sopping up every ounce of the delicious white gravy with my pan-fried goodness. It's at times like these that I remember just how versatile white gravy can be. It's amazing on top of my chicken fried steak but would be just as welcome at the breakfast table poured generously over a pile of biscuits. Even mashed potatoes can share the love of white gravy. So to add to your repertoire, I've listed the recipe for this white creamy tastiness. Feel free to pour it onto whatever suits your fancy at the time.

WHITE GRAVY

In a cast-iron skillet melt the butter over medium heat. Add the onion and cook until the onion is translucent, about 10 minutes. Add the flour and cook, stirring constantly, 5 to 6 minutes. Pour in the milk and continue cooking and stirring until the gravy thickens and coats the back of a spoon, about 4 to 6 minutes. Season with salt and pepper to taste.

Serves 2.

NOTE: For a deeper, more developed meaty flavor, use sausage or bacon fat instead of butter.

1 tablespoon butter
½ large white onion, minced
1 tablespoon all-purpose flour
1 cup milk
Salt and pepper to taste

Blue Bonnet Café

Marble Falls, Texas

Just northwest of Austin is a quaint little town known as Marble Falls, which is home to the Blue Bonnet Café. Opened in 1929, the Blue Bonnet Café has been serving up Southern hospitality, home cooking, and amazing pies since the first customer crossed the threshold. The current owners, husband and wife team John and Belinda Kemper currently run the restaurant with their daughter and son-in-law, Lindsay and David. They have stuck to the original model of giving customers a place to catch up on town news while filling their bellies with delicious goodness. Originally, the café was on Main Street, but in 1946, it moved to its current location on Highway 281.

There is something impressive about a joint that bakes its own pies daily. At Blue Bonnet Café, the pies are so popular that they actually have a pie happy hour every Monday through Friday afternoon from three to five o'clock. I have to say that sounds a lot more appealing than the happy hour specials I'm familiar with. It's definitely something I could feel happy about.

The rest of the menu is spectacular, with breakfast served all day and daily lunch specials such as chicken and dumplings, turkey and dressing, or smoked quarter chicken. And everything at the café is homemade with love you can taste. After enjoying a delicious blue plate lunch special, I was ready to satisfy my sweet tooth with some freshly baked pie. I had been eyeing them since I walked in, and although my lunch was delicious, I knew the best was yet to come.

The meringue on the tops of these pies was insane. They almost look like Bundt cakes, with giant round domes and almost three times more meringue than pie filling on the plate. It was a truly difficult decision, but since I knew my stomach wouldn't hold a piece of each kind of pie, I finally settled on the coconut cream pie. The whipped cream on top would have been enough of a treat with the yummy bits of toasted coconut, but the pie itself was divine. The coconut filling was creamy and rich, and the piecrust had just enough sweetness and saltiness to balance out the filling. I ate every last crumb and seriously considered what it would take to relocate to Marble Falls to join in on the happiness of their happy hours. Instead, I've included a recipe below that can transport me, at least temporarily, to my own personal pie happy place.

COCONUT CREAM PIE

Preheat the oven to 350 degrees.

Place 1 cup of the coconut on a baking sheet. Toast in the oven for 7 to 8 minutes, stirring halfway through the baking time, until golden-brown. Set aside to use as the topping.

In a medium saucepan, combine the sugar, flour, and salt. Stir in the milk and cook over medium heat until thickened. Reduce the heat to low and cook, stirring constantly, for 2 minutes longer. Remove from the heat and let cool slightly. Stir 1 cup of hot milk mixture into the beaten eggs. Return all to saucepan and cook, stirring, over medium heat until simmering. Reduce heat to low and cook, stirring, for another 2 minutes. Remove from the heat and add the remaining 1 cup coconut, butter, and vanilla. Stir until well blended. Pour immediately into the piecrust. Sprinkle with the toasted coconut. Refrigerate for 3 to 4 hours before serving.

Serves 8.

2 cups sweetened flaked coconut, divided

1 cup white sugar

2 ½ tablespoons all-purpose flour

⅛ teaspoon salt

3 cups whole milk

3 large eggs, beaten

2 tablespoons butter

1 ½ teaspoons vanilla extract

1 (9-inch) piecrust, baked

Bryce's Cafeteria

Texarkana, Texas

When you travel a lot, you come across some oddities. Texarkana definitely fits that description. It's not the people or the food or the culture. It's merely the fact that half of the city is in Texas and the other is in Arkansas. Because of this strange arrangement, there are several state line markers in the city where you can actually be two places at once. With its dual personalities, it was a natural stop on my Southern travels.

Bryce's Cafeteria opened in 1931 and was founded by Bryce Lawrence Sr. After forty years, it remains family-owned and -operated. The founder's sons, Bryce Jr. and Richard, now run the joint and have kept it true to its roots. At Bryce's, it's about serving up farm fresh ingredients and family recipes every day. The menu changes twice daily to keep its guests coming back.

The restaurant is set up exactly as you would imagine a cafeteria. Customers grab a tray and pick an entrée and a few sides while sliding their trays along metal shelving. It's a throwback concept, but in certain situations it's pleasantly surprising. With its Southern focus, Bryce's Cafeteria was the last place I expected to find beef enchiladas on the menu and certainly not ones worth writing home about. But I was intrigued by the odd-man-out, and it looked so delicious that I couldn't resist.

Typically, enchiladas are topped with a spicy, semisweet red enchilada sauce, but leave it to Texas to change it up. These enchiladas are covered with Bryce's special sauce—a creamy, white, cheesy enchilada sauce that will have you sopping up every last bite. The meat inside is seasoned well with just enough spice to balance the creaminess of the sauce.

The Tex-Mex surprise was a welcome addition to my list of delicious Southern must-haves, and for a place that has dual personalities, Texarkana is lucky to have such a tasty prize as Bryce's Cafeteria. The shift of gears from purely Southern to Tex-Mex came at the perfect time for my taste buds. Whether you are from Texas, Arkansas, or anywhere else, feel free to enjoy these enchiladas any time to throw you off your routine a bit.

BEEF ENCHILADAS

Preheat the oven to 375 degrees.

Place the beef in a large skillet and cook over medium heat until browned, about 15 minutes. Add the chopped onions and garlic and cook until the onions are translucent, about 10 minutes. Remove from the heat and place in a large bowl.

In a medium saucepan combine the salsa, enchilada sauce, jalapeño, cumin, salt, red pepper flakes, coriander, and sugar. Bring to a full boil over medium-high heat. Remove from the heat.

Add half of the cheese to the meat mixture and mix well. Spoon the meat mixture onto tortillas, making sure not to overfill. Roll the filled tortillas and place in a 9 x 13-inch baking dish, packing them together tightly. Pour the sauce over the top and sprinkle with the remaining cheese.

Bake for 10 to 15 minutes, until the cheese is melted and the edges of the tortillas start to brown and crisp.

Serves 6.

1 pound ground beef (80 percent lean)

½ large yellow onion, minced

3 cloves garlic, minced

3 cups jarred salsa

4 ounces jarred enchilada sauce

1 jalapeño pepper, seeds removed, chopped

1 teaspoon ground cumin

1 teaspoon salt

½ teaspoon crushed red pepper flakes

½ teaspoon ground coriander

½ teaspoon brown sugar

16 ounces shredded cheese blend (Cheddar and Monterey Jack), divided

20 (6-inch) corn tortillas

Cast Iron Grill

Lubbock, Texas

When describing a meal, people like to throw out all kinds of complimentary words to convey their experience. One of the words I often hear is "heavenly." If you are looking for a divine experience when it comes to Southern food, then you have to make a stop at the Cast Iron Grill in Lubbock. The owner, Teresa Stephens, considers running this joint her heavenly calling, and it doesn't take long to see that her heart is truly in her work.

When the restaurant opened in 2007, it was housed in an old building that became available after another restaurant closed down. The original Cast Iron Grill seated fifty-five people and was bursting at the seams after being open only five years. That's when Teresa moved the restaurant four blocks away to accommodate a much larger crowd and serve as many hungry souls as she could get her hands on. And that includes those who can't pay.

Teresa's determination to serve her community reaches past the paying customers and into the homeless community. The Cast Iron Grill is a part of Saint Benedict's Chapel homeless shelter, serving more than four hundred homeless people each month. With an owner who has a heart this big, I knew that her passion would carry over to the food, and I was right.

The Cast Iron Grill has an amazing menu that is available every day for breakfast and lunch. I happened to stumble upon this promised land on a Monday. For me, Mondays usually mean it's back to the grindstone. But walking into the Cast Iron Grill that Monday, a weight was lifted by the genuine Southern hospitality and warm smiles I encountered.

And to top it all off, the daily special was chicken spaghetti. Some of you may never have experienced the dish—it's not on any Italian menu that I'm aware of. It's usually made with a mushroom cream sauce and topped with some combination of breadcrumbs and shredded cheese. I happen to love this concoction, and as it was being carried out from the kitchen, my mouth was already watering.

I resisted the urge to dive right in, knowing full well that I had to let the delicious noodles cool a bit if I wanted to avoid scalding my mouth. After what seemed to be a reasonable amount of time, I took my first bite, and I was glad I waited. I wouldn't have wanted to miss out on any of the deliciousness on the generous plate that I was given. Once I'd licked my plate clean, I worked up the nerve to ask Teresa for her secret recipe for this delectable casserole. True to her generous nature, she obliged. Enjoy this meal with a group around the table, and the next time you're in Lubbock, be sure to stop by the Cast Iron Grill for some of the tastiest food and the nicest people you could hope to meet this side of heaven.

CHICKEN SPAGHETTI

Place the chicken breasts in a large pot and cover with water. Add ½ teaspoon of the salt and ½ teaspoon of the black pepper. Bring to a boil over medium-high heat and cook until tender and fully cooked, 20 to 25 minutes. Transfer the chicken to a cutting board, reserving the cooking liquid in the pan. Shred the chicken with a fork and let cool.

Bring the cooking liquid to a full boil over high heat. Add the spaghetti pasta and cook according to package directions. Drain the pasta and discard the stock. Set the pasta aside but do not rinse.

In the same pan, melt the butter over medium heat. Add the onion and bell pepper and cook, stirring, until tender, 6 to 8 minutes. Add the tomatoes with green chilies, soup, and shredded chicken and bring to a simmer. Add the spaghetti and stir gently. Add the cheese and stir gently to avoid breaking the noodles. Add salt and pepper to taste. Heat until the cheese is completely melted. Garnish with freshly grated Parmesan cheese.

Serves 4.

1 ½ pounds boneless, skinless chicken breasts

½ teaspoon salt, plus more to taste

½ teaspoon black pepper, plus more to taste

1 pound spaghetti pasta

½ cup (1 stick) butter

1 large yellow onion, minced

1 large green bell pepper, finely chopped

1 can tomatoes with green chilies

1 (10-ounce) can condensed cream of chicken soup

1 pound Velveeta cheese, cubed

Freshly grated Parmesan cheese

Circle Grill

Dallas, Texas

The bright yellow and red sign outside the Circle Grill in Dallas signifies a different time. It reminds me of what the signs must have looked like in the era of *Happy Days*, the popular sitcom set in the 1950s and '60s, and it towers over a small, plain building, beckoning you from the interstate highway. Walking through the front door, I half expected to see the Fonz in the corner leaning against a jukebox.

The sign is hard to miss, but even harder to miss is the delicious food that you find inside the Circle Grill. The smells from the kitchen float freely across the dining room. Like everything else in Texas, the Circle Grill is a little bit country and a little bit Tex-Mex.

I perused the menu and found many options, ranging from country-cooked specials such as chicken fried steak smothered in gravy to enchiladas smothered in red sauce. As strange as it sounds, I was drawn to the liver and onions finished off with the carrots and turnips. The liver and onions dish was delicious, but the carrots and turnips really stole the show for me.

Southerners are obsessed with taking any vegetable and turning it into a candy-sweet dish. Carrots are not exempt from this process, and I'm grateful. With their naturally sweet character, they lend themselves beautifully to the extra brown sugar or honey or whatever type of sweet substance the cook in a Southern kitchen chooses to use that day.

Turnips are another story altogether. Southern cooks know how to take the slightly bitter taste of this vegetable and combine it with just the right amount of salt and vinegar to make it so tasty you can't help but ask for seconds.

At the Circle Grill I was in for the best of both worlds with my sweet and salty accoutrements to my liver and onions. I cleaned my plate down to the last nibble, humbled myself, and practically begged for the secrets. But alas, I was met with yet another stubborn Southern holdout. I didn't let that stop me from experimenting on my own to replicate those delicious carrots and turnips. Enjoy the recipe, but if you happen to be passing through Dallas, throw on your leather jacket and penny loafers and head over to the Circle Grill for the real thing.

ROASTED TURNIPS AND CARROTS

In a large pot, combine 1 ½ gallons of the water and the salt and bring to a full boil over high heat. Add the carrots and boil until fork tender, about 15 minutes. Remove the carrots from the pan. Add the turnips to the same pan and boil until fork tender, about 15 minutes. Remove the turnips from the pan and discard the water.

Place the butter, onions, and sugar in the same pan. Cook over medium-high heat until the onions are caramelized, about 10 minutes. Add the bacon and cook until the sugary mixture caramelizes the pork fat, 3 to 5 minutes.

Return the carrots and turnips to the pan and stir to coat the vegetables evenly. Continue cooking until just before the sugar and bacon is burned, then add the vinegar and the remaining ½ cup water. Stir all the ingredients well, and cook until the liquid is reduced by half, about 15 minutes. Serve immediately.

Serves 6 to 8.

1 ½ gallons plus ½ cup water

1 tablespoon kosher salt

½ pound whole carrots, peeled

½ pound whole turnips, peeled

1 cup (1 stick) butter

1 large yellow onion, minced

1 cup sugar

¼ pound bacon, diced

½ cup distilled vinegar

Easy Street Family Café

Lewisville, Texas

The sign on the outside of the Easy Street Family Café in Lewisville has seen some better days. The place looks very unassuming from the outside—a simple main street storefront with a green tin roof awning and a faded, worn sign hanging over the front door. But when you step inside, you feel right at home, as though you've walked into someone's home. It's a small place, but big on warmth. It's the little details, such as the hand-painted bottle of Aunt Jemima pancake syrup, that caught my eye and drew me in, not to mention the delectable smells wafting my way from the kitchen.

The menu included hamburger steak, open-faced roast beef dinner, and chicken fried steak. Everything sounded delicious, but I was in the mood for something kind of different. I know this book is about Southern meat and three restaurants, but what these joints also have in common is that they serve some rockin' breakfasts. The day I stumbled upon the Easy Street Family Café, I was definitely in a breakfast mood. The decorated syrup bottle merely sealed the deal. With my mouth watering, I quickly ordered the breakfast. My plate arrived with two delicious over-easy eggs, two pancakes, home-style hash browns, and perfectly crisp bacon. With a plate like that, it was hard to pick a favorite, but the home-style hash browns stole the show.

Potatoes are somewhat of a blank canvas to me when it comes to cooking. You can transform their flavor, consistency, and crispiness into anything you want. The home-style hash browns at this little joint hit all the right notes. They were perfectly crispy and seasoned with little bits of potato skin and big chunks of potato. I was quite satisfied with my decision to veer slightly from my usual fare. I tried to pry the secret to this delicious breakfast potato concoction from the owner's hands, but I guess my sweet talk could use a little work. I've included my best effort at recreating this delicious side. But if you're in Lewisville, cruising the main drag, don't hesitate to drop by the Easy Street Family Café for a delicious breakfast, although I'm sure lunch wouldn't disappoint either.

HASH BROWNS

Preheat a large cast-iron skillet over medium-high heat and add the grapeseed oil, onions, and garlic. Add the salt and pepper and cook until slightly browned, about 8 minutes. Remove from the heat.

With a large cheese grater, shred the raw, peeled potatoes. Squeeze out the starchy liquid from the shredded potatoes and place the potatoes in a large bowl. Fold in the onion and garlic mixture.

Reheat the same skillet over medium-high heat and add 1 tablespoon of the bacon fat. When the fat is clear and smoking slightly, add the potato mixture. Press the potatoes firmly down to distribute in the pan. Cook undisturbed over medium heat for 15 minutes. With a spatula lift an edge of the potatoes to ensure they are browned, slide in the remaining 1 tablespoon bacon fat, and flip the potatoes over. Increase the heat to medium-high and cook the potatoes for 5 minutes. Break up the potatoes and cook, stirring, until the potatoes have reached the desired crispiness and are tender, about 10 minutes. Season with salt and pepper and serve. These potatoes are best served immediately.

Serves 4.

2 tablespoons grapeseed oil

1 medium white onion, minced

2 cloves garlic, minced

1 teaspoon salt, plus more to taste

Freshly cracked black pepper

4 large russet potatoes, peeled

2 tablespoons bacon fat, divided

Huck's Catfish

Denison, Texas

Rarely these days do you find a restaurant that is still operated by its original owner after twenty years, but in Denison, Huck's Catfish is still going strong under the watchful eyes of its original owner. That is enough to tell me that the restaurant must be doing something right. Huck's offers Mississippi catfish and lots of it. The staff takes pride in making sure that guests can never say they didn't get enough or the portions were too small. Serving sizes suit any waistline, from a single catfish fillet at a quarter pound all the way up to a full order of four fillets at around a pound. The fish can be fried or steamed and comes complete with your choice of two veggies.

The waitstaff explains to customers that the cooks prepare the fish light and flaky, but if the customers want it drier and crispier, they should just say, "Burn it!" The veggies offered here are plentiful and delicious. From garlic bacon slaw to old-fashioned ham and potato salad to simple sliced fresh tomatoes, this place has you covered for full-fledged yummy vegetable goodness.

Among the many sides, I was intrigued by one that I don't usually see at meat and three restaurants: pickled whole jalapeños. I am used to the vinegar-based pepper sauce placed on most tables at the standard meat and three, and if you've seen it but never tried it, I highly recommend it. It's delicious on cornbread and added to any type of beans. That being said, I just had to try the pickled whole jalapeños.

I am a fan of pickling vegetables and have been known to pickle anything from cauliflower to Brussels sprouts. When the pickling is done right, the result piques my taste buds, and I can't get enough of the sweet and sour kick with just the right amount of crispness left to the veggie. The pickled jalapeños at Huck's were a great addition to my mound of fried catfish. They were tart with a hint of sweetness and a slight crunch and just the right amount of heat teasing the back of my throat—this was a homerun! I never expected to find such delicious Delta fare so far from the mighty Mississippi, but I am glad I made the trip.

I've included a recipe for these tasty treats for you to try at home. They're a welcome addition to a delicious piece of fried fish, even if you can't rustle up some catfish. Don't let the word *jalapeño* scare you off. These peppers are truly palatable, even for those who can't handle the heat. If you can work up the nerve, I promise you won't be disappointed with the combination.

PICKLED WHOLE JALAPEÑOS

1 pound fresh jalapeño peppers

2 cups water

2 cups champagne vinegar

4 ½ tablespoons sugar

3 tablespoons kosher salt

3 bay leaves

2 tablespoons coriander seeds

5 cloves garlic, peeled

3 tablespoons mixed peppercorns

Pierce each pepper four or five times with a toothpick and place them in six 12-ounce glass preserving jars.

In a large saucepan bring the water, vinegar, sugar, salt, bay leaves, coriander seeds, garlic cloves, and peppercorns to a full boil over high heat. Reduce the heat to medium and simmer for 5 to 7 minutes. Remove from the heat and pour the mixture over the peppers. Place the lids on the jars and allow the jars and contents to cool to room temperature. When cool, refrigerate for at least 7 to 10 days before serving.

Makes 6 jars.

Southern Rose Café

Seminole, Texas

From the street the Southern Rose Café in Seminole isn't much to look at. The building is a large, rectangular, one-story building with tan paint and corrugated metal roofing. It's the unassuming locations like this one that usually catch me off guard with their delicious food, and the story is no different at the Southern Rose Café.

This Texas rose is known for its hand-breaded, deep-fried specialties such as chicken fried steak, chicken tenders, and steak fingers. The restaurant definitely has that small-town feel and offers daily specials that perpetually delight. The atmosphere is warm and welcoming.

I was caught slightly off-guard when I walked in and saw a fairly large group of people clad in the traditional Amish garb. I couldn't help but wonder if I had gotten off track and somehow ended up in Amish country. Once I got my bearings, I took a seat and perused the menu. Several things caught my eye, and I have to admit that it was a challenge to steer myself away from the hand-breaded, deep-fried traditional crowd-pleasers.

I finally settled on the stuffed chicken Milanese, a thinly sliced chicken cutlet seasoned and coated in breadcrumbs before being pan-fried. The result is a light and delicious fried chicken cutlet with loads of flavor. Traditionally, this might be served with lemon caper butter sauce, some sautéed spinach, and a side of pasta, but not here. The cooks at the Southern Rose take this delicious chicken goodness and turn it inside out. It's stuffed with the capers, sautéed spinach, and fresh pickled green tomato relish and topped with the lemon butter sauce. The result is delicious. By turning the dish inside out, the breading remains crunchy. I've included the recipe so you can recreate this dish at home and surprise your taste buds.

2 boneless, skinless chicken breasts

½ teaspoon kosher salt, divided

½ teaspoon black pepper, divided

1 teaspoon fresh lemon juice

1 teaspoon white wine

1 ½ teaspoons minced shallots

1 teaspoon sugar

1 cup dry breadcrumbs or panko

3 tablespoons grated Parmesan cheese

2 tablespoons all-purpose flour

2 egg whites

1 cup shredded mozzarella cheese, divided

4 cups sautéed spinach

1 large egg yolk

1 tablespoon olive oil

STUFFED CHICKEN MILANESE

Place the chicken breasts between two sheets of plastic wrap. Spray the plastic wrap with water to keep it from ripping. Pound the chicken to ½-inch thickness using a meat mallet or a small, heavy skillet. Season the chicken with ¼ teaspoon of the salt and ¼ teaspoon of the black pepper.

In a small bowl combine the lemon juice, wine, shallots, a pinch of salt, and sugar and stir well.

Combine the breadcrumbs and Parmesan cheese in a medium bowl. Place the flour in a small bowl. Place the egg whites in another small bowl and whisk lightly. Dredge the chicken in the flour mixture, and then dip in the egg whites. Dredge in the breadcrumb mixture on one side. Place the chicken on a baking sheet, breading side down, and refrigerate for 10 minutes.

Remove the chicken from the refrigerator. Combine ½ cup mozzarella, spinach, and egg yolk and mix well. Season with the remaining ¼ teaspoon salt and the remaining ¼ teaspoon pepper. Spoon the mixture onto the chicken. Fold the chicken over the filling and use a toothpick to seal.

Heat the oil in a large, nonstick skillet over medium-high heat. Add chicken and cook for 3 minutes. Turn chicken over and cook until browned and done, about 3 more minutes. Remove the chicken to a platter. Add the shallot mixture to the warm skillet and cook, stirring with a whisk, until reduced by one-third. Cut the stuffed chicken breasts into halves and serve with the warm shallot sauce spooned on top. Sprinkle with the remaining ½ cup mozzarella cheese.

Serves 2.

GUEST CHECK
mac
coll
rutas
swpot 175
64625
GUEST CHECK™
wht CKN 650
coll 170
yam
bep
W side of wht
wht CKN 650
limas
r/wht
64624

Index

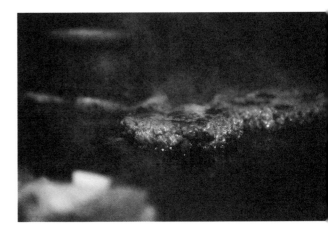

Destination Index